Maurice Cecil Mackey, Jr.
USAF Academy
15 October 1956

AMERICAN CAPITALISM

*The Concept of
Countervailing Power*

BOOKS BY

JOHN KENNETH GALBRAITH

☆

Modern Competition and Business Policy
American Capitalism

AMERICAN CAPITALISM

The Concept of

Countervailing Power

BY

JOHN KENNETH GALBRAITH

HOUGHTON MIFFLIN COMPANY BOSTON

The Riverside Press Cambridge

The Riverside Press
CAMBRIDGE · MASSACHUSETTS
PRINTED IN THE U.S.A.

For
Douglas

FOREWORD

AMONG THE PROBLEMS I encountered while working on this book, there are three which I feel justified in sharing with the reader. The first concerned the hideous threat of war. The ideas which I am here bringing to market I have been sorting out in my mind for the last three or four years. Most of them were formed, and many of them were committed to one or another of successive drafts of typescript, while it was still natural to assume that the peace would last. They deal with the United States and its economy as one was disposed to see it in the five years after the Japanese surrender. This was not a peaceful world but it was a world at peace. These ideas are not relevant to the United States at war and I would not be so bold as to suppose that they would seem very relevant when viewed from the radioactive debris that would remain after a war, including a victorious one. Not even the most unimaginative man can send a book to press in these days without wondering what the world will be like into which, after six months of gestation — three months less than a human but one month more than a goat — the helpless infant will be born. I have so wondered and it has remained only to hope. I am convinced that if my hopes are ill founded we will not in our time have a world in which speculation, of the kind on which I am here engaged, will be on such relatively amiable matters.

My second problem was much less portentous. It concerned the idiom in which one should write a book such as this. I have had, especially in the latter chapters, a great many things to say to my fellow economists. I am proud to be counted a professional economist; I consider economics a progressive as well as a distinguished subject matter. Yet I would not have written this book had I not felt that some of the conclusions now reached by my professional colleagues are quite wrong. Anyone so unfortunately persuaded should, normally, address his writing to his fellows. There are many advantages in this. Economics has developed a shorthand terminology which, however baffling it may be to the layman, has great advantages in speed and ease of communication for the initiated. It also requires a certain precision of thought and statement which is a protection against careless thinking and which places critics on firm ground in recognizing and protesting error. It also assures the critics that the author is learned in the terminology of his subject.

I must humbly appeal to the critic to believe that I could be incomprehensible had I wished, for, in spite of all these good reasons for the contrary, I have addressed this book to the layman — those, at least, who are reasonably diligent readers. There may be some — I hope not too much — that such a reader will find implausible but there will be little that he will fail to understand. I have so written because I am sufficiently confident of the ideas presented to want to seek a general audience. Also, I promised the publishers that it would be that kind of book. I am considerably in the debt of these gentlemen. Apart from some pecuniary obligations, I am indebted to them for never having asked whether it had "textbook possibilities."

In writing as I have, it has been necessary to simplify a good many matters. My competitive model is a stripped design and students of the history of economic thought will miss many refinements. I have especially simplified and abbreviated that part of the Keynesian doctrine of savings and investment which I needed for my purpose. But simplification can be of two kinds. It can be a matter of convenience which leads to conclusions that are based on the full content of truth. Or it can lead to error. My simplification is intended to be of the first sort. If any is of the second sort I expect to be held accountable.

Third, I have had to contend, as I imagine have many others, with the problem of how to designate, with reasonable brevity, the differing political attitudes of Americans on economic issues. In a book like this the line between economics and politics must truly be an imaginary one — it is a parallel that must be crossed and recrossed without consultation even with the reader. In the United Kingdom there are Socialists and Tories and when one uses these political labels to designate a group of people one indicates fairly accurately the political views and temperament of those designated. Needless to say, with us party labels convey no similar meaning. The term Republican combines a reference to Senator Wayne Morse and Mr. Herbert Hoover; both Senator Harry Flood Byrd and Ambassador Chester Bowles are within the limits of irregularity permitted to a Democrat.

In our time the ancient and useful distinction beween Left and Right has developed a color which also makes it nearly useless. To many the notion of the "Left" connotes some alignment, direct or vague, with communism and in any case there is an older tendency to associate it with political positions derived from Marx. The Right for many has become synonymous with blind reaction. Accordingly these terms bear not on the reality but the pathology of our political life and with the latter I am not much concerned.

My solution has been to follow W. S. Gilbert and classify all men as liberal or conservative — if not by birth at least by temperament and the effects of circumstance. This, at least, has the sanction of long usage. So far as the American conservative is concerned, it presents no serious difficulty. American conservatism has the unifying characteristic of dislike of change. It does divide as to tactics — as between those who resist change *qua* change, which is perhaps the normal pattern of our conservatism, and those who accept limited change to protect the broad contours of the past and present.

The use of the term liberal raises far more questions — almost as many as it answers. In Europe the term has a clear political content: the Continental liberal is, and simply, an opponent of government intervention in the economy. In practice, this means resistance to any interference with vested positions of privilege or monopoly as well as to any and all forms of state-sponsored planning. There are Americans who regard themselves as liberals in this sense, but not many. American liberalism is far more likely to view improvement in welfare and also an attack on vested position as its central tasks and to accept, or indeed seek, whatever state intervention it believes to be required for these ends. The best one can do with the term, as we use it, is to assume such an attitude coupled with a general predisposition toward change. After all, it is one of the distinctive features of American liberalism, that on economic matters both its methods and its goals are exceedingly diverse. When a basket is filled with a great many different kinds of vegetables, one cannot strain to say that it contains only potatoes.

Let me add, finally, that I think the reader will find this a good-humored book. There is a place, no doubt, for the great polemic — for the volume that assails with unmitigated fury the ideas, interests, morals and motives of all unfortunates, the quick and the dead, who happen to be in the author's path. I am not capable of such anger; I would like to suppose that I do not take myself so seriously. In any case this is a method which probably serves better the purposes of politics and evangelism than of enlightenment.

Yet this is an essay in social criticism. The task of criticism is criticism. I pass under review ideas that are strongly held and positions that are warmly defended and, with some, at least, I take vigorous issue. Even though they are, as here, the ideas men respect, this is the way of progress. And such criticism is especially important in economics. Like theology and unlike mathematics, economics deals with matters which men consider very close to their lives. There has always been a tendency for its ideas to crystallize into dogma; neither liberals nor conservatives have a very good record of weighing challenges to accepted concepts and doctrines with critical detachment. Accordingly, one of the most important and difficult of the responsibilities of the economist is to resist the authority of the accepted.

CONTENTS

AMERICAN
CAPITALISM

The Concept of
Countervailing Power

CHAPTER I

The Insecurity of Illusion

IT IS TOLD that such are the aerodynamics and wing-loading of the bumblebee that, in principle, it cannot fly. It does, and the knowledge that it defies the august authority of Isaac Newton and Orville Wright must keep the bee in constant fear of a crack-up. One can assume, in addition, that it is apprehensive of the matriarchy to which it is subject, for this is known to be an oppressive form of government. The bumblebee is a successful but an insecure insect.

If all this be true, and its standing in physics and entomology is perhaps not of the highest, life among the bumblebees must bear a remarkable resemblance to life in the United States in recent years. The present organization and management of the American economy are also in defiance of the rules — rules that derive their ultimate authority from men of such Newtonian stature as Bentham, Ricardo and Adam Smith. Nevertheless it works, and in the years since World War II quite brilliantly. The fact that it does so, in disregard of precept, has caused men to suppose that all must end in a terrible smash. And, as with the bee, there is deep concern over the intentions of those in authority. This also leads to apprehension and insecurity.

It is with this insecurity, in face of success, that this book, in the most general sense, is concerned. The favorable per-

formance of the American economy in the years following
World War II is a fact. There were some two million farm
families, many of them in the Southern Appalachians, who
continued to live in a primitive and anonymous squalor not
surpassed in any country west of Turkey. There were urban
slum dwellers and racial minorities, notably the Negroes, who
could not view their lot with satisfaction. The same was true
of those whose salaries, pensions or dependence on past savings committed them to life on a fixed income. Elsewhere
there was little hardship. Nor, so far as one can judge, did
the generality of Americans feel that their personal freedom
had been seriously abridged. The ideas which caused the
present to be viewed with such uncertainty, and the future
with such alarm, were not operative. My purpose is to see
why — and perhaps to learn how, if we are spared — these
ideas can be kept inoperative in the future.

II

That there was deep uneasiness over the economy in this
time is a point that need hardly be labored. Undoubtedly it
was greatest among businessmen. The five years following
World War II were ones of high production and generous
profits. Business had recovered much of the prestige it had
lost during the depression; except at election time it was
again being treated with marked courtesy by the government.

Yet there was little evidence that businessmen, or more
especially their leaders, viewed their prospects with equanimity. On the contrary the tone of business statements during these years was often that of a communiqué promising a
last-ditch stand against disaster. Thus, in early 1948 the

weekly organ of the nation's leading business organization, the *NAM News*, observed that the President's State of the Union Message promised "impossible burdens" for business and quoted, approvingly, the view of unnamed conservative politicians that, if enacted, the program "would first hobble and then ultimately destroy the American business system." A few weeks later, in March, the same journal reported that the president of the Association had taken to the road to spread "industry's ideas and ideals in the unremitting battle against totalitarianism." This it should be noted was totalitarianism at home, not abroad, and having carried his "plea for freedom" to Kansas City he proceeded to Houston, Shreveport and New Orleans where he warned that the "threat to American freedom is unremitting." A year later his successor told a Jacksonville audience that "at the highest level of prosperity, our people have lost faith in freedom and are moving away from it." An Association editorial somberly observed that "millions who yield to no one in their zeal to advance the national welfare are seriously concerned lest what we struggle against on a world-wide basis creep upon us at home without our realizing it. They believe we will drift into Statism. . . . " President Truman's new message to the Congress was subsequently viewed with alarm. Early in 1950 the Chamber of Commerce of the United States, in an attractively printed brochure entitled *Socialism in America*, warned, urgently, against the "back road to socialism." It drew attention to the then recently expressed fears of Mr. James F. Byrnes, former Supreme Court Justice, Senator and Secretary of State, that the people of the United States could "be led over a bridge of socialism into a police state."

This pessimism is subject to considerable discount even by businessmen themselves. On April 21, 1950, at a luncheon meeting in Baltimore the President of the United States Steel

Corporation made the apocalyptic declaration that the American economic system was "in deadlier peril than it has ever been in my lifetime." The stock market rose moderately in late trading and Steel Common was up a quarter for the day. A prominent business spokesman conceded at the 1949 meeting of the National Association of Manufacturers that businessmen were in the vanguard of gloom. The people, at large, he declared, were "apathetic and complacent . . . too busy playing golf, or looking at television, or tending to their businesses, to protect the freedom and opportunity which have made America what it is."

Yet the notion that American capitalism [1] is a fragile and evanescent thing has a strong grip on the minds of many citizens. The principal, and apart from treason the all but exclusive, issue in elections since the war has been whether America is being transformed from a capitalist into a Welfare state, a Statist state, or a Socialist one. Early in 1950 the Republican Party formally resolved to fight its next election campaign on the issue of "liberty versus socialism." The Honorable Jesse W. Wolcott of Michigan was able to give a precise arithmetical measure to the imminency of revolution. "The United States is now within 8 per cent of socialism," he told an audience of realestate men in late 1949. The President of Columbia University, in sending his flock into the world in 1949, was less quantitative but scarcely less urgent. "In the years ahead of you graduates, the fundamental struggle of our time may be decided — between those who would further apply to our daily life the concept of individual free-

---

[1] For many years this term, which denotes that the men who own the business, or those who are directly or indirectly their agents, have a major responsibility for decision, has been regarded as vaguely obscene. All sorts of euphemisms — free enterprise, individual enterprise, the competitive system and the price system — are currently used in its place. None of them has the virtue of being more descriptive and none is as succinct.

dom and equality; and those who would subordinate the individual to the dictates of the state. . . . "

III

The businessman has shared with many others yet another fear which, unlike his political doubts, he has left largely unexpressed. It is that private capitalism is inherently unstable. For full five years after the Japanese surrender in 1945, nearly every mature and prudently conducted business in the United States was guided by the assumption that, at some time in the future, the United States would have a serious depression. The postwar inventory, dividend and reserve policies of American corporations and the jagged behavior of the stock market in face of record incomes and yields become comprehensible only when the depth and breadth of this alarm is recognized.

In accordance with a surprisingly well-observed convention, the American business spokesman does not often express his fear of depression in public. To express the fear is, perhaps, to invite the fact — and perhaps also to inspire the interest of the state in measures to counter the threat. Few others have been under such a ban. Farmers, workers and intellectuals, in the years following the war, made no secret of their fear of depression. Before the war ended it was taken as accepted that there would be a postwar collapse with unemployment ranging upward from seven, eight or ten millions. What was called postwar planning consisted almost exclusively in planning for such a disaster. The postwar guarantees of farm prices, the large public-works programs that were projected and the Employment Act of 1946 all tacitly assumed such a collapse.

The case of the farmers has been especially instructive. For five years following the war Congress was almost continuously concerned with farm legislation, immediate or prospective. During these years very few farmers — very few, at least, of those whose voices are heard in Washington — were dissatisfied with the prices and incomes they were receiving. On the contrary these were bonanza years such as few had ever dreamed. But it was taken for granted by farmers that American capitalism would one day return to its normal pattern of performance. For most this was a simple portrait of its behavior during the nineteen-thirties. To protect themselves in that collapse of capitalism, they were enthusiastically advocating and enacting the comprehensive controls over their price and production which conservatives saw as the antithesis of capitalism.

IV

The liberal, since the end of the war, has shared, and has not hesitated to voice, the conservative's conviction that American capitalism is unstable with a strong bias toward depression. He has had further causes for disquiet. As the conservative has worried about government power so the liberal has been alarmed over business power. In what I shall presently argue is a normal pattern of capitalist organization, a large share of the productive activity of the United States is carried on by a comparatively small number of corporations. Agricultural production, much trade and, subject to some underlying administration by trade unions, the mining of soft coal and the manufacture of clothing are still in the hands of the small firms. Much though not all of the rest is in the domain of the giants; the heads of the corporations that produce between a third and a half of the national product of the United States could be seated comfortably in almost any neighborhood motion-picture theater.)

This is not new. It is possible that the hundred largest corporations did nearly as great a proportion of all the business of the United States in 1905 as today. It was only in the thirties, however, that the extent of this concentration was measured with passable thoroughness. The statistics converted what had been a suspicion into a conviction.

There is no place in the liberal's system for these vast administrative units. The large corporation can have significant power over the prices it charges, over the prices it pays, even over the mind of the consumer whose wants and tastes it partly synthesizes. There is nothing in the American tradition of dissent so strong as the suspicion of private business power. It produced the Sherman Act, a nearly unique effort to shape the growth of capitalism, the Wilsonian efforts to extend its effectiveness, the colorful lawsuits of Thurman Arnold in the late thirties, and the liberal lawyer's undiluted enthusiasm for antitrust enforcement.

In spite of all these efforts — and apparently the statistics now left no room for comforting disbelief — big business had triumphed. No plausible doctrine was available, even to conservatives, which led to the conclusion that the undisturbed exercise of its power would be for the common good. On the contrary the accepted doctrine held that, via monopoly, it led to social inefficiency and to oppression. The optimism of the American liberal as to what might be accomplished by the antitrust laws has always been great. For the first time it now became necessary for him to wonder if even the antitrust laws could alter the existing structure of the American economy. If not, big business and its power were here to stay. To his uneasiness over power for which he had no rationalization, the liberal was forced to add a further component of despair.

V

Here then is the remarkable problem of our time. We find ourselves in these strange days with an economy which, on grounds of sheer physical performance, few are inclined to criticize. Even allowing for the conformist tradition in American social thought, the agreement on the quality of the performance of American capitalism is remarkable. The absence of any plausibly enunciated alternative to the present system is equally remarkable. Yet almost no one feels secure in the present. The conservative sees an omnipotent government busy altering capitalism to some new, unspecified but wholly unpalatable design. Even allowing for the exaggeration which is the common denominator of our political comment and of conservative fears in particular, he apparently feels the danger to be real and imminent. At any given time we are but one session of Congress or one bill removed from a cold revolution. The liberal contemplates with alarm the great corporations which cannot be accommodated to his faith. And, with the conservative, he shares the belief that, whatever the quality of current performance, it is certain not to last. Yet in the present we survive. With the present, given peace, no one is intolerably unhappy.

It can only be that there is something wrong with the current or accepted interpretation of American capitalism. This, indeed, is the case. Conservatives and liberals, both, are the captives of ideas which cause them to view the world with misgivings or alarm. Neither the structure of the economy nor the role of government conforms to the pattern specified, even demanded, by the ideas they hold. The American government and the American economy are both behaving in brazen defiance of their rules. If their rules were binding, they would already be suffering. The conservative, who has already had two decades of New and Fair Deals would already be dispossessed. The liberal, who has already lived his entire life in an economy of vast corporations, would already be their puppet. Little would be produced; we should all be suffering under the exploitation and struggling to pay for the inefficiency of monopoly. The fact that we have escaped so far means that the trouble lies not with the world but with the ideas by which it is interpreted. It is the ideas which are the source of the insecurity — the insecurity of illusion.

CHAPTER II

The Foundations of the Faith

THE LATE Lord Keynes, in what promises to be the most widely quoted passage from his pen, observed that "the ideas of economists and political philosophers, both when they are right and when they are wrong, are more powerful than is commonly understood. . . . Practical men, who believe themselves to be quite exempt from any intellectual influences, are usually the slaves of some defunct economist." Although ideas underlie the uneasiness described in the last chapter, it would be wrong to suppose they are the sole explanation. Something must be attributed to mere reaction to change. The well-to-do and the wealthy man will normally be mistrustful of change. This has been so, in the past, in nearly all times and places. It is a simple matter of arithmetic that change *may* be costly to the man who has something; it cannot be so to the man who has nothing. There will always be a high correlation between conservatism and personal well-being.

Generalizing more broadly, as the United States proceeds to higher levels of well-being, there is certain to be a steady retreat from social experiment. Indeed, were it not dangerous to extend a trend derived from only one brief decade of prosperity, one could argue that this rejection of social experiment is already far advanced. American liberals have

11

made scarcely a new proposal for reform in fifteen years. It is not evident that they have had any important new ideas. Reputations for liberalism or radicalism have now come to depend almost exclusively on a desire to finish the unfinished social legislation of the New Deal. It was adversity that nurtured this program; with prosperity social invention came promptly to an end. On domestic matters, liberal organizations can no longer be said to have a program. Rather they have a file. Little is ever added. Platform-making consists, in effect, in emptying out the drawers. The Midwest and Great Plains, which two decades ago provided Congress with its most disturbing radicals, now returns its staunchest conservatives including several of its most determined reactionaries. The political destiny of the United States does not rest with those who seek or who are suspected of wishing to repeal laws, withdraw services and undo what has been done. This also is change and unwelcomed. But given peace and prosperity it no longer rests with those who advocate major social experiment. In a country where well-being is general, the astute politician will be the one who stalwartly promises to defend the *status quo*.[1]

II

The ideas which are the deeper cause of insecurity are the common heritage of liberals and conservatives alike. These

[1] I sense, for example, that the unexpected strength of the Democrats in 1948 lay not with Mr. Truman's promise of any great forward steps in economic policy but in his evident willingness to defend what existed including the measures enacted in the New Deal years. The Republican Party, by contrast, was handicapped by the suspicion — which numerous of its spokesmen and supporters reinforced rather than dispelled — that it harbored a deep nostalgia for the past and might seek change in that direction.

derive from a theory of capitalism which has deeply shaped the attitudes of both. This is the system of classical economics which was constructed in the latter part of the eighteenth and during the nineteenth century, primarily in England. Those who would make its acceptance a test of sound Americanism should know that, to a singular degree, it is an alien doctrine. Its principal early architects were Englishmen and Scots. American economists, although they added some important amendments and reproduced it in countless textbooks, contributed comparatively little to the structure itself. Until fairly recent times Americans have not shown high originality in economic theory, and the habit of looking abroad for authority is still strong. It was the classical system, as imported from nineteenth-century England, that became the explicit and remains the implicit interpretation of American capitalism.

The bearing of this system on the insecurity stressed in the last chapter becomes evident, even in cursory view, when it is examined in relation to the world it is presumed to interpret. Given this system, or more accurately, an economy constructed to its specifications where there is stout observance of its rules of behavior, all of the worries of the preceding chapter dissolve. It described an economic system of high social efficiency — that is to say one in which all incentives encouraged the employment of men, capital and natural resources in producing most efficiently what people most wanted. There could be no misuse of private power because no one had power to misuse. An innocuous role was assigned to government because there was little that was useful that a government could do. There was no place in the theory for depression or inflation. The system worked. This was the promise, but it was a promise made only to a society with the proper economic institutions and the proper respect for the rules of behavior which the classical system required. In the contemporary United States few of the preconditions for the system can seriously be supposed to exist. Nor do we pretend to live by its rules. Accordingly, it can only be assumed that we stand constantly in danger of reaping the terrible reward of our neglect and our disobedience. The dangers and even the disasters we risk are no less fearsome because we do not know their precise shape or why they do not come.

III

The first requirement of the classical system, as everyone is aware, is competition. In the design of the system this was fundamental and, if it was present in a sufficiently rigorous form, it was also sufficient. In practice, another condition, more properly an assertion, was added in the form of Say's Law of Markets. This held that the act of producing goods provided the purchasing power, neither too much nor too little, for buying them. Thus there was invariable equivalence between the value of what was produced and the purchasing power available to buy that production. It will be evident, even from the most casual reflection, that this comforting doctrine went far to preclude either a serious depression or a violent inflation.

The kind of competition that was necessary for this system was rigorous or, rather, there was a tendency to specify an increasingly rigorous form of competition with the passage of time. The classical economists — Adam Smith, Ricardo and Mill — were not especially self-conscious in their use of the term. Competition was the rivalry of the merchants of the town or of the cotton manufacturers or pit proprietors of nineteenth-century England. Adam Smith contented himself with distinguishing competition from monopoly by its consequences: "The price of monopoly is upon every occasion the highest which can be got. . . . The price of free competition, on the contrary, is the lowest which can be taken, not upon every occasion indeed, but for any considerable time together." [2] But toward the end of the nineteenth century, writers began to make explicit what had previously been implied; namely, that competition required that there be a considerable number of sellers in any trade or industry in informed communication with each other. In more recent times this has been crystallized into the notion of many sellers doing business with many buyers. Each is well informed as to the prices at which others are selling and buying — there is a going price of which everyone is aware. Most important of all, no buyer or seller is large enough to control or exercise an appreciable influence on the common price. In the language of the most distinguished modern exponent of the classical system as an economic and political goal, "The price system will fulfill [its] function only if competition prevails, that is, *if the individual producer has to adapt himself to price changes and cannot control them.*" [3] The rigor of this definition of competition must be stressed especially to the business reader, for it has been the source of an endless amount of misunderstanding between businessmen and economists. After spending the day contemplating the sales force, advertising agency, engineers and research men of his rivals the businessman is likely to go home feeling considerably harassed by competition. Yet if it happens that he has measurable control over his prices he obviously falls

[2] *Wealth of Nations* (London: P. F. Collier & Sons, 1902 ed.), vol. 1, pp. 116–17.

[3] F. A. Hayek, *The Road to Serfdom* (Chicago: University of Chicago Press, 1944), p. 49. The italics are mine.

short of being competitive in the foregoing sense. No one should be surprised if he feels some annoyance toward scholars who appropriate words in common English usage and, for their own purposes, give them what seems to be an inordinately restricted meaning.

Yet the notion of a market for an industry in which no producer or buyer has *any* influence on price is not as improbable as appears at first glance. There is no wheat or cotton grower in the United States whose contribution to the wheat or cotton market is appreciable in relation to the total supply. In January 1949, a Missouri cotton planter made what was believed to be the largest sale of cotton in the history of the Memphis spot market. But the 9400 bales he sold for $1,400,000 was an almost infinitesimal six tenths of one per cent of the 1949 supply. This planter could have gone to heaven with his cotton instead of to Memphis and there would have been no noticeable tremor on any earthly market.

So it is with most other agricultural products. In the nineteenth century, when the classical system was taking form, agriculture contributed a considerably larger share of the national product than at present. Moreover the burgeoning cotton industry, coal-mining and metal and metal-working industries of England of the time were all shared by numerous producers. The production of each was small in relation to that of all. None could much influence the common price. Finally, in England of the day sellers were exposed to prices that were made in the markets of the world at large. The kind of competition that was implicit in the pioneering designs of the classical economists of the nineteenth century was not unrealistic. It described a world that existed; those who formulated the theory were practical men.

This did not remain the case. Economists, as noted, in

seeking to give precision to their language, added rigor to the notion of competition. They also began to require of competition a meaning which would cause it, in turn, to produce the economic and social consequences which earlier economists had associated with it. The definition of competition was gradually accommodated to the requirements of a model economic society; it became not the definition that described reality but the one that produced ideal results. The preoccupation ceased to be with interpreting reality and came to be with building a model economic society. The definition of competition was, in effect, accommodated to the requirements of that model. Its nexus with the competition of the real world, which itself was in process of change, was no longer maintained.

By the early decades of the present century the task of constructing this model of a capitalist society regulated by competition was virtually complete. It was an intellectual achievement of a high order. As a device, in theory, for ordering the economic relations between mankind, it was very nearly perfect. Socialist theorists — Enrico Barone the great Italian scholar and Oskar Lange the equally notable Polish economist — used the theoretical performance of the competitive model as the goal of a socialist state. Few of the original architects of the competitive model would have defended it as a description of the world as it is — or was. For some the competitive model was a first approximation to reality — it departed from real life only to the extent that there was monopoly in industry or over natural resources, including land, or that government or custom interposed barriers to competition. For others it was the goal toward which capitalism might be expected to move or toward which it might be guided or a standard by which it might be appraised. For yet others the construction and refinement of the competitive model was a challenging intellectual exercise.

The birth, development and subsequent career of an idea is something like that of a human. The parents have measurable control over the first two stages but not the third. Once constructed, the competitive model passed into the textbooks and the classrooms. In the absence of any alternative interpretation of economic life, it became the exclusive system of all who undertook to teach economics. It was and remains the economics of those who essay to popularize the subject — to instruct in one lesson. The qualifications, and especially the warnings that there had been an abstraction from reality, were lost or neglected. To this day the abstraction, largely undiluted and unqualified, is the principal residuum of the considerable expense that has gone into the effort to teach economics to Americans.

Man cannot live without an economic theology — without some rationalization of the abstract and seemingly inchoate arrangements which provide him with his livelihood. For this purpose the competitive or classical model had many advantages. It was comprehensive and internally consistent. By asserting that it was a description of reality the conservative could use it as the justification of the existing order. For the reformer it could be a goal, a beacon to mark the path of needed change. Both could be united in the central faith at least so long as nothing happened to strain unduly their capacity for belief.

It is now necessary to examine the performance of the model in more detail.

IV

The notion of efficiency as applied to an economic system is many-sided. There is the matter of getting the most for the least — the commonplace engineering view of efficiency. There is also the problem of getting the particular things that are wanted by the community in the particular amounts that they are wanted. In addition some reasonably full use must be made of the available, or at least of the willing, labor supply. There must be some satisfactory allocation of resources between present and future production — between what is produced for consumption and what is invested in new plant and processes to enlarge future consumption. There must also be appropriate incentive to change — the adoption of new and more efficient methods of production must be encouraged.

Finally — a somewhat different requirement and one that went long unrecognized — there must be adequate provision for the research and technological development which brings new methods and (though one is permitted to deplore them on occasion) new products into existence. All this makes a large bill of requirements.

The peculiar fascination of the competitive model was that, given its particular form of competition — that of many sellers, none of whom was large enough to influence the price — all the requirements for efficiency, with the exception of the very last, were met. No producer — no more than the Kansas wheat grower of fact — could gain additional revenue for himself by raising or otherwise manipulating his price. This opportunity was denied to him by the kind of competition assumed, the competition of producers no one of whom was large enough in relation to all to influence the common price. He could gain an advantage only by reducing cost. Were there even a few ambitious men in the business he would have to do so to survive, for if he neglected his opportunities others would seize them. If there are already many in a business it can be assumed that there is no serious

bar to others entering it. Given an opportunity for improv-
ing efficiency of production, those who seized it, and the
imitators they would attract from within and without, would
expand production and lower prices. The rest, to survive at
these lower prices, would have to conform to the best and
most efficient practices. In such manner a Darwinian struggle
for business survival concentrated all energies on the reduction of costs and prices.

In this model, producer effort and consumer wants were
also effectively related by the price that no producer and no
consumer controlled or influenced. The price that would
just compensate some producer for added labor, or justify
some other cost, was also the one which it was just worth the
while of some consumer to pay for the product in question.
Any diminution in consumer desire for the item would be
impersonally communicated through lower price to producers. By no longer paying for marginal labor or other
productive resources the consumer would free these resources
for other and more wanted employment. Thus energies were
also efficiently concentrated on producing what was most
wanted.

In the competitive model these changes did not raise the
threat of unemployment. When the tastes of the consumer
waned for one product they waxed for another; the higher
price for the second product communicated to the producers
in that industry the information that they could profitably
expand their production and employment. They took in the
slack that had been created in the first industry. Even had
the consumer decided to save, the saving was for investment
— for another kind of expenditure. In any case it was always
open to the worker in this system to insure his own employment. Any particular employer was restrained from expanding employment only because the outlay for the added

employment was not covered by the resulting increase in income at the going price. The worker seeking employment had it within his own power to alter this delicate balance by offering to work for a lower wage. By doing so he could always make it worth the while of an employer to give him a job. A union, by restraining this wage-cutting, could obviously do damage in this delicately adjusted Elysium. But unions were not a part of the system.

v

There was never full agreement among the architects of the model on the manner in which labor and the other productive resources of the community were allotted as between consumption and investment — between current use and the production of plant, equipment, utilities and public works which would yield their return only over a period of time in the future. However, despite sectarian disputes on details, there was something close to a consensus on the nature of the underlying process. Here as elsewhere competition rendered efficient service. The competition of those who sought the prospective return from plant, machinery, utility or other investment established a price, in the form of the rate of interest, for those who were willing to save from current consumption and thereby make these investments possible. A high return from additional investment would bid up the price for savings. This would lead to more savings and less current consumption. Resources would thus be freed for investment. By the same process the community's desire for goods for current consumption would be balanced against the prospect of having more and different goods as the result of investment

If it is assumed that immediate consumption is man's normal preference, and that he will only save if he is paid to do so, it is wholly unnatural to suppose that anyone would first deprive himself of consumers' goods and then, by not turning over his savings for investment, deprive himself also of the reward for his thrift. Accordingly, whether a man consumed or saved, his income was in either case spent. But even the stubborn hoarder — and no one was quite so scorned by the ninetenth-century builders of the competitive model — did no irreparable damage. By getting income and neither spending it nor allowing others to do so he withheld some demand from the market. The only effect of this was that the impersonally determined prices for goods fell as supply exceeded demand. Others then found their current income buying more than before. Their spending offset the additions to the miser's hoard.

Here was the basis of the notion that there could never be an excess of savings — that the aggregate of demand for all goods must always equal their supply. This was Say's Law — the claim upon immortality of Jean Baptiste Say, the French interpreter of Adam Smith. Few ideas have ever gripped the minds of economists so firmly as Say's Law; for well over a hundred years it enjoyed the standing of an article of faith. Whether a man accepted or rejected Say's Law was, until well into the nineteen-thirties, the test of whether he was qualified for the companionship of reputable scholars or should be dismissed as a monetary crank.

Say's Law reinforced the conclusion that, in the competitive model, there would always be full use of willing labor. As a result, to the extent that the model was taken to be an approximation to reality, no serious consideration could be given to the possibility or fact of a bad depression. A depression must involve some interruption in the flow of spending

— some general reduction in demand for goods below the capacity of the economy to supply them. What is being spent at any given time for consumers' goods is obviously being spent. Interruptions between the receipt of income and its ultimate disposal must be sought for in that part of income that is saved. But Say's Law arrested any search for trouble in this area by declaring that savings or their equivalent must also be spent. A decrease in expenditures by consumers would only mean an increase in saving and investment expenditure. Under such circumstances it was impossible to suppose that a general and progressive reduction in spending — without which there could be no depression — could get under way.

There was room in this system for rhythmic cycles of good business and bad. So long as the principal effect of such movements was on profits and the rate of economic growth, rather than on employment, no serious collision with Say's Law occurred. And, in fact, the business cycle became the object of a good deal of statistical study, especially in the United States. Much data could be gathered, and many charts could be drawn without trespassing on Say. But until the mid-thirties, in both England and the United States, the notion of the grave depression was not only foreign to the accepted system of economics but its admission was largely barred to analysis. Unemployment, which was sufficiently a fact so that it could not be ignored, was generally associated with the activities of unions. Unions prevented the worker from getting himself employed by preventing him from reducing the wage at which he offered to work and so making it worth the while of an employer to hire him. This was not the dogma of mossbacks; it was the only important avenue to an explanation left by Say and the competitive model. As late as 1930, Sir William Beveridge, a modern symbol of unorthodoxy, firmly asserted that the effect, at least potentially, "of high wages policy in causing unemployment is not denied by any competent authority." [4]

Say's Law and the resulting sterility of the interpretations of business fluctuations helps explain the rather passive role played by economists in the very early years of the Great Depression. Many men of reputation either said nothing or vigorously but unhelpfully condemned unbalanced budgets or relief to farmers, businessmen, banks and the unemployed.[5] Politics, in all cases, dictated another course — and the judgments of politicians not of economists, as viewed in retrospect, reflected the course of wisdom. Fortunately the economists were soon to be rehabilitated by the intellectual repeal of Say's Law.

To return to the competitive model. Clearly it either solved the operating problems of the economy, including the great questions of social efficiency, or, as in the case of the severe depression, it excluded the problem from consideration. Efficiency in its various forms was assured by the pressure on the individual firm to produce cheaply, to keep abreast of others in progress, and by the role of an impersonally determined price in passing gains along to consumers and in passing their demands back to producers. The same price structure, abetted by flexible wages and a theory which

[4] He subsequently continued: "As a matter of theory, the continuance in any country of a substantial volume of unemployment which cannot be explained by specific maladjustments of place, quality and time, is in itself proof that the price being asked for labour as wages is too high for the conditions of the market; demand for and supply of labour are not finding their appropriate price for meeting." William Beveridge, *Unemployment* (New York: Longmans, Green & Co., 1930), pp. 362–71.

[5] Especially in the field of monetary policy the initiative passed to men who were not beholden to Say's Law because they had not worked in the main stream of economic theory. This was true, for example, of the late Professor George F. Warren of Cornell, the author of the famous gold buying policy.

identified the act of saving with the fact of investment, went far to preclude unemployment. Say's Law canonized the doubtful points. It is already easy to understand the depths of the nostalgia for such a mechanism, however rigorous its requirements. It is also possible to understand how the conviction that its rules were being violated, or the admission that the model could never be achieved in practice, could leave a community, which had long used this system as a reference point in interpreting its economy, with a sense of profound disquiet.

CHAPTER III

The Problem of Power

ITS SOLUTION of the problem of efficiency was what commended the competitive model to the economist. Efficiency has long been a near fetish of economists and, in the beginning, there was a strong humanitarian basis for this preoccupation. Until the nineteenth century, grinding poverty had at all times and in nearly all places been the fate of all but a minority of mankind. For the relief of this poverty, nothing could be quite so important as to get more production from existing manpower and resources. Indeed, in a world where there was little unemployment, no other remedy for poverty was available given current income distribution and the considerable political discomfort and frustration that was frequently the fortune of those who advocated more equitable distribution of income. The prospect of alleviating poverty, Marshall observed, "gives to economic studies their chief and their highest interest." [1]

For the businessman and the political philosopher, by contrast, the appeal of the competitive model was its solution of the problem of power. This is still the basis of its hold on the American conservative. Indeed, for most Americans free competition, so called, has for long been a political rather than an economic concept.

[1] Alfred Marshall, *Principles of Economics* (New York: MacMillan Co., 1920, 8th ed.), p. 4.

The role of power in American life is a curious one. The privilege of controlling the actions or of affecting the income and property of other persons is something that no one of us can profess to seek or admit to possessing. No American ever runs for office because of an avowed desire to govern. He seeks to serve — and then only in response to the insistent pressure of friends or of that anonymous but oddly vocal fauna which inhabit the grass roots. We no longer have public officials, only public servants. The same scrupulous avoidance of the terminology of power characterizes American business. The head of the company is no longer the boss — the term survives only as an amiable form of address — but the leader of the team. It is years since the United States has had a captain of industry — the brass-bound officer who commands has now been entirely replaced by the helmsman who steers. No union leader, John L. Lewis excepted, ever presents himself as anything but a spokesman for the boys.

Despite this convention, which outlaws ostensible pursuit of power and which leads to a constant search for euphemisms to disguise its possession, there is no indication that, as a people, we are averse to power. On the contrary few things are more valued, and more jealously guarded by their possessors, in our society. Prestige in Congress is nicely graded to the number of votes the particular member influences or the potency of his committees. The amount of authority a public servant exercises or — a rough index of this in the lower reaches of the public service — the number of people working under his direction, are the accepted measure of his importance in Washington. It is taken for granted in the public service that both authority and subordinates will be eagerly accumulated by the energetic man.

Prestige in business is also associated with power. The income of a businessman is no longer a measure of his achievement; it has become a datum of secondary interest. Business prestige, as a moment's reflection will suggest, is overwhelmingly associated with the size of the concern which the individual heads. American business has evolved a system of precedence hardly less rigorous than that of Victorian England. It is based almost exclusively on corporate assets. In the business peerage the ducal honors belong to the heads of General Motors, Standard Oil of New Jersey, Du Pont and the United States Steel Corporation. The earls, baronets, knights and squires fall in behind in reasonably strict accordance with the assets of their respective firms. In our time the man who is merely rich is of little consequence. Homage is, to be sure, paid to the "small but successful" businessman. But the very form of the phrase shows that he has had to surmount the handicap of being small to earn his place in the sun.

The reason is not that the business community pays single-minded obeisance to corporate size and therewith to the men who head the largest concerns. Rather it is that the size of the corporation which the individual heads is again a rough index of the power the individual exercises. With size goes the ultimate responsibility for the decisions affecting the largest number of employees, over prices that affect the largest number of customers, over investment policies which work the greatest change in the income, livelihood or landscape of the community. While the individual must disavow his interest in making such decisions, his colleagues in the respect they accord him, show as clearly as do Congressmen and public servants in their respective fields the direction of their own ambitions.

II

Power obviously presents awkward problems for a community which abhors its existence, disavows its possession, but values its exercise. In the nature of man, the alarm over the exercise of such power runs to second persons. The businessman is not disturbed about the use of authority of which, by hard work and merit, he has become the custodian; he is alarmed about its misuse by government. The liberal naturally views the exercise of private power with concern. Given public office he is not likely to be persuaded of the danger of misusing his own righteously won authority. This tendency to alarm over the possession of power by second persons is greatly enhanced by the convention of denying that one possesses power. The conventional assertion that one has none is readily translated into belief. In any case, the man who is possessed of authority, private or public, is always likely to be more conscious of the checks and reins on his decisions than of his power to reach them. A decision which one is free to make rarely impresses one as an exercise of power. To the extent that it makes any impression at all it is likely to seem a rather obvious exercise of intelligence. A decision on which one is blocked by the authority of another is a very different matter. It is bound to make a deep impression. The impression will also, normally, be one of arbitrary or egregious misuse of power. This is why we live in a world of constant protests against the authority of others and of replies which reflect a deep and usually genuine content of injured innocence.

The competitive model provided an almost perfect solution of the problem of power as aggravated by these conventions and attitudes. Given its rigorous prescription of competition, there was very little scope for the exercise of private economic power and none for its misuse. And with the private exercise of economic power so circumscribed, there was no need for public authority to regulate it. Specifically, if no business is large enough to influence prices on the market in which it sells or on the market in which labor or materials are bought, no one can do anything very harmful to consumers, suppliers or wages of workers because no one has any power over prices charged or prices or wages paid. The man who is moved to exploit his consumers through unduly high prices will survive only long enough to discover that they have deserted him in favor of his numerous competitors. To pay a worker less than the going wage is to invite him to go where the going wage is paid. It requires only a moment's reflection to conclude that a businessman with power neither to overcharge his customers nor to underpay his labor (and for similar reasons his other suppliers) has very little power to do anybody ill.

To minimize the exercise of private power, and especially the opportunity for its misuse, was to remove most of the justification for exercise of government authority over the economy. It is unnecessary for government to control the exercise of private power if it does not exist in any harmful form. And since the efficiency of the economic system is already at a maximum without government interference, it must be presumed that any intervention of government would reduce efficiency. In a state of bliss, there is no need for a Ministry of Bliss.

III

In the competitive model, intervention by the state in the economy was excluded with equal rigor whether the motives of the state were assumed to be malevolent or benign. The model was formulated in a day when good intentions by the state and its servants could not be assumed. The most vigorous of the political philosophers associated with its design, Jeremy Bentham, sought for nothing so eagerly as to minimize the role of corrupt public officials. There was good reason for this. Until well into the nineteenth century in England, and well into the present century in most of the rest of the western world, the motives of the state authority, in relation to the economy, were at least episodically rapacious or corrupt. Even in the United States, until the present century, the federal government was the patron, in economic matters, of those best situated for extracting favors and of its own employees.

The doctrine of the malignant state is not quite dead. A recent treatment of the American economy concludes that, through progressive income taxation, the government more or less deliberately "deprives its successful citizens of their product and gives it to the less successful; thus it penalizes industry, thrift, competence, and efficiency, and subsidizes the idle, spendthrift, incompetent and inefficient. By despoiling the thrifty it dries up the source of capital, reduces investment and the creation of jobs, slows down industrial progress . . ." [2] Not even the intentions of Jackson could have been viewed more dismally by a Boston merchant. But there can be little doubt that this is a minority view. In the United States, as in the parliamentary democracies in general, the great majority of the people have come to regard the government as essentially benevolent. To the extent that the New Deal in the United States had revolutionary significance

[2] *The American Individual Enterprise System. Its Nature, Evolution, and Future.* By The Economic Principles Commission of the National Association of Manufacturers (New York: McGraw-Hill Book Co., Inc., 1946), p. 1019.

the revolution was in attitudes of the great masses of the people toward the federal government. Within the span of a few years a comparatively detached and impersonal mechanism, hitherto identified with tariff-making, tax-collecting, prohibition, Farmer's Bulletins and the National Parks, came to be regarded as a protector and even as a friend of the people at large. The actions of the government might not be considered entirely predictable but there was no doubt that its motives were thought good.

However, the competitive model also excluded power that was exercised in the name of welfare and good intentions. Well intentioned or not, such intervention was at best redundant and at worst harmful. This explains why, among those who interpret the world by the competitive model, the epithet "do-gooder" can be one of greater opprobrium than "evil-doer." It also explains their alarm as changing attitudes have swept the state into activities inconsistent with its role in the model.

IV

For a community that finds power agreeable in the first person and abhorrent in the second, the competitive model gave men of striking differences in viewpoint a strong unity of purpose. All could find within it a program suited to their temperament and interest. Thus for the businessman it provided a strong justification for resisting the intrusions of government. It also provided an answer to those who suggested that *he* had undue power. Competition denied it to him; his seeming power was a mirage. Better aware than anyone else of the restraints on his decisions, he could believe it. His critics cherished the competitive model because it denied power both to the entrepreneur and to government. They could suspect the businessman of possessing economic power but their remedy was only to have a purer form of the same kind of economy as the businessman himself espoused.

It is scarcely surprising that many men continued to cling to the competitive model as an idea long after its substance had seemingly deserted them.

Nor can it be supposed that faith in a system of ideas which seemed to solve so many problems could disintegrate without important consequences. But it has disintegrated. This has been partly the result of changes in the underlying reality. To a much greater extent it has been the counterpart of the process by which the competitive model was built. What was elaborated in the world of ideas could be destroyed in the world of ideas; what economists gave they could take away. Since it was not the economy so much as the ideas that changed, the consequences, happily, have been less physical than psychological, less of the stomach than of the mind. To the process of disintegration and its consequences I now turn.

CHAPTER IV

The Abandonment of the Model

THE SYSTEM of ideas just outlined — the theory of capitalism and the solution of the problem of power it provided — was vulnerable at two points. In the realm of ideas there was its pivotal dependence on competition, on a definition of competition that had tended to become increasingly precise and hence increasingly brittle. Even the staunchest defenders of the doctrine required a rigorous form of competition — with Professor Hayek they held that it had to be the competition in which "the individual producer has to adapt himself to price changes and cannot control them." [1] There was also, in the world of reality, the need for performance. The system had to work. Were the assumption of competition to be undermined, it would be a devastating blow. So, equally, would be a failure in performance. Both blows fell simultaneously in the decade of the thirties.

The first blow had been in the making for many years — that it would come sooner or later was implicit in the pattern of industrial growth that has occurred both in the United States and throughout the western world. With many notable exceptions — agriculture, the textile and garment industries, soft-coal mining, wholesale and retail trade, shoe manufacturing — the number of firms participating in a business is

[1] See page 15.

likely to be at its maximum within a few years or even a few
months after the business is born. Thereafter there is, typically, a steady decline until a point of stability is reached
with a handful of massive survivors and, usually, a fringe of
smaller hangers-on. Thenceforward the changes in the industry are in the relative positions of the established firms. This
is not a universal pattern of development but it is a typical
one. The automobile, steel, rubber, farm implement, tobacco,
liquor, chemical and radio industries all took such a course.
Of the several-score firms now making television sets, there is
a good chance that all but a handful will disappear within
the next decade.

The process by which the typical industry passes from the
hands of the many to the few has not been well understood.
Not infrequently in the United States it has been identified
with a design by someone to acquire monopoly control of enterprise. There have been spectacular searches for the devils.
The Muckrakers and the Pujo investigation of 1912 looked
for the *deus ex machina* of the consolidation movement of
the preceding decades — and thought they found it in the
bankers. (These were the years which produced International Harvester, International Nickel, International Paper,
International Silver and International Salt, as well as the
more modestly titled United States Steel, all attesting by their
names the generous horizons of the men who put them together.) In the thirties the Pecora investigations and the Temporary National Economic Committee looked, somewhat less
specifically, for the architects of the utilities combines, the
big motion-picture companies, the theater chains and the
burgeoning chain store systems.

To regard the tendency toward concentration of ownership in an industry as the result of some individual's imperial
design is to miss the point. In fact, the causes are deeply

organic. Except in industries where the maximum advantages of size are realized at a relatively small volume of production — agriculture, some types of trade, and some few fields of mining and manufacture — entry into an industry is easy only when it is very new. Then the recruitment of capital by all is based on hope and promise and it is impossible to distinguish the promise of an embryo Ford from that of an embryo Preston Tucker. No aspirant has the advantage of organization and experience; none has achieved the status of a comparatively sure thing. Since all are beginners all are small, and the capital requirements for any one are modest.

With the growth of the industry the firms already in operation also grow. In doing so they realize whatever technical economies there may be in larger-scale production and the successful ones also acquire, either directly from earnings or from their reputation for making them, the wherewithal in new capital for further growth.

These firms also acquire — a point somewhat neglected by economists — the economies of experience. The development of an industrial enterprise is a fairly intricate task in organization and administration. It can only be accomplished easily when it is accomplished slowly — when there is opportunity to search for talent, to try new men out a few at a time, and when there is leisure to reassign, promote to innocuousness, or detach with regrets, the inevitable mistakes. Only a little of this can be afforded at any given time.

The result is a passive but highly effective handicap on the latecomer. In this race the horse with the poorest record, or no record, must carry the greatest weight. Capital must be found in spite of the fact that there are other firms that are a better prospect for the investor. In recent times the Reconstruction Finance Corporation has eased the problem of entry of new firms and it is indeed significant that the new arrivals in such industries as automobile, steel and aluminum production in the last ten years have all had capital from this source. But even if the aspirant has the necessary merit and friendships to obtain government funds he must still contend with new foremen and untried supervisors and engineers and he must risk the *gaucheries of* untried executives. An old firm may have a few neophytes; the new firm has few others. It must accomplish, often in a few months, the tasks of organization which those already in the field have worked out, step by step, over many years. As a result, in an established industry, where the scale of production is considerable, there is no such thing as freedom of entry. On the contrary, time and circumstances combine to bar the effective entry of new firms.

At the same time that entry becomes difficult or impossible, the forces which tend to reduce the number already in the industry continue. Weaklings may still fail, and disappear, especially in bad times. Good times make it easy to finance consolidations and tempting for the strong company to expand and the weak to sell out. Thus, both depression and prosperity work, alike, to reduce the number of firms in an industry. The combination of a low or zero birthrate and a continuing death rate must always be a declining population.

The growth pattern here described is not peculiar to the United States. Industrial development appears to have followed a roughly similar path in other advanced countries. There may, however, be something distinctive about the final equilibrium in the United States. In Western Europe the end result, abetted by cartel agreements, has frequently been a single massive survivor or combination. With us it is far more typically a few large firms together with a fringe of small ones. This equilibrium is apparently associated with a certain equality of strength among the major survivors coupled with a measure of equality of size that makes it difficult for any one large firm to buy another out. At this stage, too, consolidation is consolidation of giants. It has become a sufficiently massive and spectacular affair so that public opinion and the possibility of adverse attention from the Department of Justice both act as deterrents. At the same time the price competition of the large firms is likely to be sufficiently circumscribed by caution so that the smaller fringe can live, albeit often precariously, under the umbrella the large firms provide.

Having reached this stage, little further change occurs in the membership of the typical industry. There is no more cherished view of the American economy than that which regards it as a biological process in which the old and the senile are continually being replaced by the young and vigorous. It is a pleasant but almost certainly a far-fetched fiction. In fact the present generation of Americans, if it survives, will buy its steel, copper, brass, automobiles, tires, soap, shortening, breakfast food, bacon, cigarettes, whiskey, cash registers and caskets from one or another of the handful of firms that now supply these staples. As a moment's reflection will establish, there hasn't been much change in the firms supplying these products for several decades.

II

An economy where the typical industry is shared by a few firms is awkwardly inconsistent with a theory of capitalism which requires that power to affect prices or wages or output or investment be impersonally governed by the reactions of the many. During the thirties, as the result of a singularly important series of studies, the notion that there was extensive concentration in American industry gained wide acceptance. The first of these studies was the epochal investigation by Adolf A. Berle and Gardiner C. Means into the proportion of national wealth, industrial wealth and corporate assets owned by the two hundred largest non-financial corporations.[2] This was followed by further investigations under government auspices by Means,[3] more yet by the Temporary National Economic Committee and, since World War II, still further studies by the Federal Trade Commission and the Department of Commerce.

Three questions were at issue in these studies, namely: how important are a minority of very, *very* big corporations in the American economy? To what extent are markets divided between a relatively small number of large firms — large, that is, in relation to the markets they share? Does concentration become greater year by year?

There is still something less than complete agreement on the answers and not all of the discussion which these studies have provoked has been of Olympian objectivity. The government, so often inclined in economic matters to assert that all is for the best in the best of all worlds, has, in this case, shown no disposition to minimize the extent of the concentration or the need for vigorous counteraction through the antitrust laws.[4] The critics of the figures have, with a few exceptions, been men who are deeply devoted to the economic and political system identified with the competitive model as an economic and political goal. They have been in the always equivocal position of the man who must testify to the virtue of a well-loved mistress.

---

[2] *The Modern Corporation and Private Property* (New York: Commerce Clearing House, Inc., 1932; and Macmillan Co., 1932).

[3] *The Structure of the American Economy. Part I. Basic Characteristics. National Resources Planning Board* (Washington: U.S. Government Printing Office, 1939).

[4] See the reference to the Federal Trade Commission study below.

Yet the principal conclusions, if stated with reasonable moderation, are not subject to serious challenge and have gained wide acceptance. The importance of the large corporation, and the large proportion of manufacturing, transportation, utilities service and mining which a comparatively small number perform, is clear. Means calculated [5] that for 1933 the 200 largest non-financial (i.e., producing or controlling as distinct from financing) corporations and their subsidiaries had approximately fifty-seven per cent of the total assets of such corporations. A recent investigation by the Federal Trade Commission shows, for the year 1947, that the 113 largest manufacturing corporations owned forty-six per cent of the property, plant and equipment employed in manufacturing.[6]

Whatever the margin of error in these figures, it cannot be great enough to alter the essential conclusion which is that a small number of large corporations are responsible for a very substantial proportion of all industrial activity. And, in fact, this conclusion has not been seriously challenged.

That the typical industry is shared by a relatively small number of corporations — that there is concentration in individual markets as well as in the aggregate — has provided more opportunity for debate. So, also, have the attempts to show that concentration is increasing year by year. With reference to the latter the evidence is, in fact, decidedly dubious. It may well be that the appearance of new industries — television, air freight carriage, specialized gambling

---

[5] *The Structure of the American Economy, loc. cit.*

[6] The Federal Trade Commission, *The Concentration of Productive Facilities, 1947* (Washington: U.S. Government Printing Office, 1949). However other types of assets, notably inventories and cash, are also indispensable for operations and there is some evidence from Means' earlier studies that to confine the comparison to physical assets is to maximize the concentration ratio that is shown. (Cf. *Structure of the American Economy*, p. 107.)

services are notable post-World War II examples — is sufficient to offset the consolidation that goes on within older industries.

The measurement of the concentration within industries has run afoul of the imprecision of the word industry. As this term is used in everyday discourse and as it is used for statistical purposes, it groups together the production of some highly unrelated products and it runs boundaries between products that are closely interchangeable. Crosleys and Cadillacs are both products of the automobile industry, but a cut in price or a doubling of output of Crosleys is not a datum of perceptible importance to the Cadillac Division of General Motors. Copper, brass and aluminum, which are closely interchangeable for many uses, are products of different industries. Withal, the notion of an industry as a group of firms supplying roughly the same market has practical usefulness and it would be impossible to get along without it.

In spite of these problems, which have provided an almost unparalleled opportunity for quibbles,[7] these studies affirm, at least, that over an important sector of the American economy individual markets are shared by a small number of producers. In the production of motor vehicles, agricultural machinery, rubber tires, cigarettes, aluminum, liquor, meat products, copper, tin containers and office machinery the largest three firms in 1947 did two thirds or more of all business. In steel, glass, industrial chemicals, and dairy products the largest six accounted for two thirds. There is a similar degree of concentration in a host of less important or derivative industries. And in a number more — gasoline, cement,

[7] For an interesting and competent one, see Clair Wilcox, "On the Alleged Ubiquity of Oligopoly," *Papers and Proceedings of the American Economic Association*, May 1950, pp. 67 ff.

mixed fertilizer and milk distribution — markets that are necessarily regional or local are typically divided between a similarly small number of sellers.[8]

There are numerous industries where the number of firms serving the same market remains large and where no one or no small number have any considerable proportion of the total business. But for a large and important sector of the economy — indeed for the industries which are commonly supposed to typify American capitalism — this is clearly not the case. On the contrary, as one of the leading contemporary students of market organization has concluded, "The principal general indications of studies of American market structure are [among others] that concentration of output among relatively few sellers is the dominant pattern." [9] The acceptance of such a conclusion could not but be damaging to a theory of capitalism based on the notion that markets were shared by many producers no one of them large enough to influence the common prices paid or received.

III

Meanwhile economic theory, as distinct from economic statistics, had also dealt the competitive model a serious blow. Economists had anciently recognized one major exception to the competition of the many. That was the limiting case of monopoly — the case where one firm was in complete control of all the product of an industry. So long as economists held to this bipolar classification of industries — competition *or* monopoly — the position of competition as a valid assumption concerning the economy was relatively secure.

---

[8] Federal Trade Commission, *op. cit.*

[9] Joe S. Bain in *A Survey of Contemporary Economics* (Philadelphia: Blakiston Co., 1948), p. 136.

That was because monopoly — the absolute monopoly of the single firm — was so rare as to have the standing only of a curiosity. Apart from the public utilities there was, before World War II, only one example that could easily be brought to mind, namely the Aluminum Company of America.[10] So long as monopoly was so exceptional, competition must be the rule. The economy as a whole must be competitive.

In 1932–33, under the combined attack of an American and a British economist (Professor E. H. Chamberlin of Harvard University [11] and Mrs. Joan Robinson of Cambridge University [12]) the old bipolar classification of markets, competition *or* monopoly, was abandoned. New categories of markets, neither purely competitive nor fully monopolized, were recognized between the two. In this intermediate zone were industries whose markets had the characteristics of both competition and monopoly. They were monopolistically or imperfectly competitive.

The establishment of a multiple, rather than a double classification of markets was the most far-reaching contribution of the new theory. It meant, although it wasn't wholly foreseen at the time, the end of the faith in competition in the old sense. Now there were alternatives to the implausible assumption of competition without going to the implausible case of monopoly. The competition of many sellers, like the control of a market by one, soon came to be regarded as an extreme or limiting case. From the statistical investigations as well as from everyday observation it was evident, moreover, that one of the intermediate types of markets — that of

[10] Which now, of course, shares the ingot market with the wartime arrivals.

[11] *The Theory of Monopolistic Competition* (Cambridge: Harvard University Press, 1932).

[12] *The Economics of Imperfect Competition* (London: Macmillan Co., 1933).

few sellers or oligopoly as it came to be called — was of
commanding importance. No sooner had oligopoly been recognized as something different from either competition or
monopoly than it was on its way to replace competition as
the principal assumption by which the industrial economy
was interpreted.

However, a vast distance separates oligopoly from the
competition of the competitive model. Price-making in markets where there are a few sellers is not only measurably influenced by the actions of any individual firm but the individual must take into consideration the response of others to
his initiative. If he correctly appraises what is advantageous
for the industry as a whole, the others presumably will follow
his lead. Otherwise they will not. When each seller considers
the advantage of any action from the viewpoint of the profits
of the industry as a whole he is obviously thinking much as
would a monopolist. To assume that oligopoly was general
in the economy was to assume that power akin to that of a
monopolist was exercised in many, perhaps even a majority
of markets.

In actual practice things are both simpler and more complicated. They are simpler because in most industries where
there are few sellers there soon develops a tacit understanding which allows one firm to assume some measure of leadership. This firm makes an appraisal of the price policy that
is appropriate for itself with greater or less consideration of
what will be acceptable to the other members of the industry.
The others follow its lead. Things are more complicated because, except under conditions of very strong demand, any
firm in an industry can initiate price reductions. This normally forces others to follow suit. There is no similar compulsion to follow a price increase. Any one of the large cigarette companies can bring down cigarette prices by lowering

its own price. It cannot as certainly bring the others up by raising its prices. As compared with monopoly, one of the mitigating facts about oligopoly is the commanding position of the firm which sees the greatest advantage in low prices.

Price-making under oligopoly is further complicated by the fact that there is never complete substitutability between the products of different sellers. A Ford differs from a Chevrolet and the differences are energetically magnified by the advertising of the companies. This gives to Ford and General Motors a measure of independence in their prices. The same is true, though in small degree, even of chemically identical products like steel or sulphur. Habit, corporate personality, terms and promptness of delivery will hold customers even in face of minor price differentials.[13] However, these are details. The important thing is that the doctrines of a monopolistic or imperfect competition paved the way for a destruction of the old assumption of competition on which the competitive model was erected. It is now time to see what took its place.

IV

It is a measure of the magnitude of the disaster to the old system that when oligopoly or crypto-monopoly is assumed it no longer follows that any of the old goals of social efficiency are realized. The producer now has measurable control over his prices. Hence prices are no longer an impersonal force selecting the efficient man, forcing him to adopt the

[13] Economists have commonly worked with a category of markets described as "undifferentiated" or "pure" oligopoly. In principle, as in fact, no such category exists. If the number of sellers is small they will always be identified as distinct personalities to the buyer. And although their products may be identical, their personalities will not and cannot be.

most efficient mode and scale of operations and driving out the inefficient and incompetent. One can as well suppose that prices will be an umbrella which efficient and inefficient producers alike will tacitly agree to hold at a safe level over their heads and under which all will live comfortably, profitably and inefficiently. There is no longer, by the old line of argument, any certainty of technical advance. When there are many producers in an industry, some one of them will certainly seize upon any known innovation. In so doing, the pioneer forces others to follow. To resist progress is to perish. If there is only a handful of producers, there is a chance that none will assume the initiative. There is at least the possibility that all will prefer and concur in choosing profitable stagnation.

When sellers have gained authority over prices, prices no longer reflect the ebb and flow of consumer demand. It was such price movements in the competitive model which equated consumer desires — as evidenced by their willingness to pay — with what producers found it worth while to supply. When prices are tacitly administered by a few large firms they no longer move freely and production no longer responds automatically to price changes. An increase in demand may bring increased production at the old prices; it may just as well lead to a decision to increase prices and profits with production remaining as before.

In any case it must be assumed that prices will be set and production will be managed, however imperfectly, with an eye to the profits of the industry. One of the oldest conclusions of economics is that a price so set — a monopoly price — must be higher and the resulting output smaller than under conditions of competition. Thus not only does oligopoly lead away from the world of competition, with its promise of efficiency, but it leads toward the world of monopoly.

This, anciently, had been viewed as the very antithesis of social efficiency.

There were other bitter consequences of the new assumptions. A close examination of oligopoly showed that price competition, the very motor of the competitive model, was not only sharply circumscribed but had to be. ⟨When there are only a few firms in an industry and their products are closely substitutable, a price cut by one company must, as just noted, be matched by the others. Otherwise the firm with the lower price will draw a disproportionate share of the business in the short run and, through operation of habit and customer good will, may well retain it in the long run. This the other firms must prevent. An aggressive and persistent price-cutter can, accordingly, affect the level of prices and return of the entire industry. Should he persist and provoke retributive action, the ensuing price warfare can be ruinous to all. There is no point set by cost or any other consideration below which prices cannot go. Cuts must be matched and, if the game is fully played through, all can be ruined. ⟩

Businessmen who live in the shadow of this disaster, as do all who share markets with a few firms, protect themselves by a convention. This convention simply outlaws the use of prices as a weapon of competitive warfare. The convention against price competition, when there are only a few sellers in a market, is a matter of great importance. It is also so much a part of customary business practice that where it is well observed its very existence is often unnoticed even by those who adhere to it. Prices continue to change and they may be changed, at the instance of an aggressive and efficient leader, when that firm knows that the result will be uncomfortable for other firms. But this is very different from using prices as a sanguinary weapon for invading another's markets or separating him from his customers. This the convention prohibits and there is nothing more frightening, in industries where the convention is not rigidly observed, than the news that a price war has broken out. Quite typically the individual who resorts to price competition does so surreptitiously and the opprobrious character of his action is suggested by the terms in which he is normally described: he is irresponsible, a chiseler, an unfair competitor, a man who is guilty of unsound or even un-American business practices. The primitive defender of the convention against price competition does not hesitate to use racial epithets to assail the unorthodox competitor.

Nevertheless, the convention against price competition is inevitable under oligopoly. The alternative is self-destruction, which cannot be expected of men with a normal desire to remain solvent and which in any case would serve no useful purpose. Although the structure of the market of small numbers precludes aggressive price competition — the uninhibited price movements which the competitive model requires — economists have been reluctant to concede the fact. They have regularly rebuked the businessman who foreswears price competition as a traitor to the price system. The businessman has been understandably mystified by these attacks. Evidently the test of his faith in competition is his willingness to court disaster in its name.

The final embarrassment from the unraveling of the new ideas was that as price competition in its pristine form disappeared, other forms of competition became suspect. The convention against retributive price competition in the market shared by a few large firms does not extend to other forms of commercial rivalry. Individual firms retain their desire to keep and even to enlarge their share of the market. The first is important for survival, the second for both profits and prestige. With price competition ruled out, competitive

energies are normally concentrated on persuasion and, especially in consumers' goods, on salesmanship and advertising.
The cigarette manufacturer recruits customers, not by the
self-defeating and dangerous device of cutting cigarette prices
but, with the unreluctant aid of his advertising agency, by
recourse to the radio, billboards and television screens and
through magazines and the press. This is competition but no
longer the kind of competition that is eligible for a blanket
defense. On the contrary, the very instrument which once
rewarded the community with lower prices and greater efficiency now turns up assailing its ears with rhymed commercials and soap opera and rendering the countryside hideous
with commercial art. What hath Adam Smith wrought?

In any case no one could any longer argue very seriously
that the cost and volume of even the comparatively inoffen-
sive forms of competitive selling and advertising were in
response to popular demand. Not only had the old pressure
for efficiency in production been lost, but there appeared to
be a positive premium on expenditures on distribution. This
was all readily assimilated to the new theory. Indeed, given
the market of the few it was normal and natural.

One consequence of the new ideas was to place economic
theory sharply in opposition to the burgeoning advertising
industry. Not unnaturally, those advertising men who take
their profession seriously, and have the normal human wish to
be wanted, have not found it pleasant to be considered ex-
traneous. Since they were hardly in a position to devise a
new system of theory which would re-establish their place
in the scheme of things, they have been reduced to stating,
often with some vigor, that it is advertising that made this
country what it is today. Perhaps it was a mark of their good
nature that they weren't more put out with economists than
they were. The adman was one of the many displaced per-

sons who was caught up in the retreat from the competitive model.

v

Such was the general state of ideas on economic efficiency in the main tradition of economics — in the impeccable line of descent from Adam Smith, Ricardo and Alfred Marshall — at the beginning of World War II. Such, with relatively few modifications, is where the main ideas concerning what economists call value or market theory remain today. By evolution, from a system where nearly everything worked out for the best, economists found themselves with a system where nearly everything seemed to work out for the worst.

It would be a mistake to exaggerate the alarm with which the generality of economists viewed this result. One author did go so far as to plead with his colleagues "to recognize that the concept of a system of monopoly is self-contradictory and the very negation of everything economics stands for." [14] They were adjured to see no evil. In a great personal tragedy, Heinrich von Stackelberg, a brilliant German contributor to the new theory, apparently lost all hope of any order in the economy except as might be provided by the state. Almost alone among the German economists of any distinction he became an active National Socialist.

A certain number of economists have also undertaken to revive the faith of their colleagues in the existence, actual or potential, of the competition of the competitive model. But even this task has been assumed, in the main, by popular writers whose faith in pure competition has not been weakened by contact with the new ideas.

[14] Eduard Heimann, *History of Economic Doctrines* (New York: Oxford University Press, 1945), p. 219.

This philosophical detachment of the economists is to be explained by their much greater interest in the last fifteen years in the problem of depression and by their preoccupation with factors bearing more directly on the total performance of the economy. Nonetheless the new market theory had a profound effect. A generation ago American economists, an inconvenient bias toward free trade apart, were counted among the staunchest allies of the businessman and among the nation's most notable defenders of the *status quo*. Partly as the result of the new ideas, they have since acquired an almost unexcelled reputation for waspishness. The very term economics has come to be identified in the minds of many conservatives, if not with radicalism, at least with an inordinate capacity to find fault. This by itself is of little consequence, and in any case, men who afflict the comfortable serve equally with those who comfort the afflicted. One cannot suppose that American capitalism would long prosper without the critics its leaders find such a profound source of annoyance. Nonetheless, the new ideas had the far-reaching consequence of bringing into question a basic supposition of capitalism — the supposition of efficiency. They are the first of the causes of insecurity which it is the task of this essay to isolate.

CHAPTER V

The Rebirth of Market Power

THE OLD SOLUTION of the problem of economic power suffered the same devastation from the new measures of market concentration and the new ideas as did the old confidence that social efficiency would be maximized. The competition of the competitive model solved the problem of private economic power by denying it, at least in a dangerous form, to anyone. The exception was the rare case of the monopolist. He did have plenary authority over his prices and production and therefore over the wealth and welfare of some part of the community. It was agreed by everyone, the monopolists themselves excepted, that such power was evil and that it should be struck down or be made subject to regulation by the state wherever it was found. The regulation of monopoly represented one of the few instances where, given the competitive model, it was agreed that the state would have to exercise its authority in the economy.

If there are only a handful of firms in the typical industry, and if they recognize their interdependence, as they must both for profit and for survival, then privately exercised economic power is less the exception than the rule in the economy. It is also of a piece with the power anciently associated with monopoly. This was the clear conclusion of the new ideas. And the fact of such power, once identified by the theory, could readily be verified by observation. The executives of the United States Steel Corporation, the longtime price leaders in the steel industry, do have authority to raise and lower the prices they charge for their own steel. When they exercise that power the industry normally follows. The same executives make decisions on where to build new plants and how much plant to build, what to pay in dividends and, subject to an annual trial of strength with the union, what wages to pay. They have considerable latitude on all of these matters; they are not the automatons of market forces. These decisions also affect the wealth and income of hundreds of thousands of people. As with steel so with the great core of American industry. The new theory suggested the existence of such power; the eye confirmed it.

Nothing could be more disturbing, in light of long-standing attitudes toward private economic power and the inflammatory connotation long given to the term monopoly, than the realization that economic power belonging to the *genus* monopoly was commonplace in the economy. Yet such power was now brought nakedly into view. Its existence was affirmed by the statistics and its nature was identified by the theory. This has all come about in the last fifteen years. No one, neither economist nor businessman, liberal nor conservative, has quite known what to do about this flauntingly indecent exposure.

II

In the American liberal tradition, a finding that private economic power exists has been tantamount to a demand that it be suppressed. As long as economic power was associated with monopoly in the old sense, the liberal had a ready-made formula. He could demand prosecution of the offending monopoly under the Sherman Anti-Trust Act with a view to its dismemberment or, if this latter were impractical as in the case of the utilities, he could advocate public regulation or public ownership. So long as monopoly was considered an exception in a world of competition — a small tumor in a mass of healthy tissue — this was a reasonably practical program. The number of targets inviting attack was not too great; a vigilant government could be expected to police competition and keep it free.

The notion that there are aspects of monopoly in a large proportion of American industries was bound to bring a major change in liberal attitudes. In fact, it dealt the ancient liberal formula a far more serious blow than has even yet been realized. It is possible to prosecute a few evil-doers; it is evidently not so practical to indict a whole economy. So, where there had once been reasonable agreement among liberals that the antitrust laws were the heart of their program, something like a three-way split appeared. There were those who did conclude, without too much reflection on the task they were setting for themselves, that the weapons for attacking monopoly would also serve against oligopoly. There were others who concluded that some form of government regulation, generally rather ill defined, would have to assume a task which the antitrust laws could no longer perform. Still others looked at the competition of the giants to see if they could not find something, however removed from the competition of the model, which could still be deemed "workable." The common feature of all three enterprises has been a very large component of frustration.

The first reaction, in point of time, was to urge more vigorous enforcement of the antitrust laws against the newly recognized and now ubiquitous monopoly power. As the

significance of the new statistics on industrial concentration
came to be appreciated in Washington in the late thirties,
there was a sharp increase in interest in antitrust enforcement.
Thurman Arnold, who was to become the most energetic
and successful trust-prosecutor the country has had, was
brought to that post in 1938. Appropriations of the Antitrust Division of the Department of Justice under his leadership were increased from $435,000 in 1936 to $1,325,000
in 1941. (They amount now to nearly four million.) One of
Arnold's cases, that against the large tobacco companies
finally decided by the Supreme Court in 1946, also appeared
to give a handle for dealing with oligopoly. There was no
proof that these firms had entered into any overt agreement
on prices. This had been the old test of guilt. Rather, each
had merely behaved as though it fully understood and respected the welfare of the group. The leadership of one of
their number had been accepted when it was evident that a
price decrease would be to the profit of all, and again when
it was evident that a price increase would be to the common
benefit. Their conviction for such behavior, the commonplace behavior of firms when the industry is shared by a few
giants, was upheld.[1] This was indication that the old weapon
against monopoly could be brought to bear on oligopoly.[2]

However, sober consideration was fairly certain to suggest
that the effect of the new ideas, by making monopoly diffused and commonplace rather than specific and exceptional,

[1] It was not completely commonplace, for the common reduction in
price, which occurred in 1933, came at a time when the ten cent or economy brands were making deep inroads into the sales of the majors. Prices
were advanced in 1934 when this threat had receded. This timing undoubtedly impressed the courts. *American Tobacco Co.* v. *United States.*
328 U.S. 781 (1946).

[2] For an exuberant but very competent expression of the optimism with
which this case was greeted see Eugene V. Rostow, *A National Policy for
the Oil Industry* (New Haven: Yale University Press, 1948), pp. 123 ff.

was to weaken the faith in the old liberal program. Even a successful prosecution, unless it results in a complete break-up of existing firms, does not alter the fundamental behavior patterns of the industry. So long as there are only a few massive firms in an industry, each must act with a view to the welfare of all. They cannot, by force of law, be made to act as though they had no economic power — as though each were insignificantly small. The leading student of the industry has observed that the big tobacco companies, after they had been prosecuted (and rather modestly fined), continued "to follow essentially the same . . . price policies . . . they followed before."[3] This was also the subject of bitter complaint before, and by, a Congressional committee in 1948.[4]

In fact, for Chesterfields, Lucky Strikes and Camels to be in active price competition would be highly inconsistent with the theory by which the market for this product is interpreted. The theory suggests that when the price of one brand changes all must change, or the leader must rescind his move. And the theory correctly interprets the case. Not only is this what has happened but it is the only thing that can happen. Each firm has to consider its actions in light of the responses of the other two. There cannot at the same time be independence and interdependence, and interdependence is the nature of things. As a practical matter in the tobacco business the letter of legality could apparently be met by the companies by maintaining small differences in the wholesale price of cigarettes — differences too small to be reflected to the consumer or to make much difference in the margin of the retailer.[5] Not a great deal else has been changed by the case against the

[3] William H. Nicholls, "The Tobacco Case of 1946," *Papers and Proceedings of the American Economic Association*, May 1949, p. 289.

[4] "Monopolistic and Unfair Trade Practices," House Report 2465, 80th Congress, 2d Session, December 1948, p. 11.

[5] Nicholls, *op. cit.*

companies, and will not be so long as three companies have a commanding position in the market.

The tobacco companies — and oligopolies generally — could, of course, be dispersed into many small units. However, American courts have been notably cautious in the remedies they have invoked under antitrust laws. Decrees dissolving existing companies or forcing them to divest themselves of subsidiaries have been exceedingly and increasingly rare. The order divorcing the manufacture of railroad equipment from Pullman car operation has been one of the few of its kind in the past twenty years. However revolutions are brought about, it is not by litigation.

Thus, while the liberal could hope that the occasional monopoly might be broken up he can scarcely suppose that the antitrust laws are an effective instrument for dispersing the economic power implicit in oligopoly. To suppose that there are grounds for antitrust prosecution wherever three, four or half dozen firms dominate a market is to suppose that the very fabric of American capitalism is illegal. This is a notion which can seem sensible only to the briefless lawyer. Yet, to repeat, the interpretation of this market leads relentlessly to the conclusion that the power exercised by a few large firms is different only in degree and precision of its exercise from that of the single-firm monopoly. And clearly it is a lot more important. The liberal, who still searches for old-fashioned monopoly in the modern economy, has been made to feel that his is a search for poison ivy in a field of poison oak.

The evident alternative to competition is public regulation or planning. This has long been supposed to be the only alternative. Under the pressure of the new ideas some American liberals have turned consciously to this alternative. "Striving after individual competition as a neat self-regulating device is fruitless because, by its nature, it cannot be established and maintained by law. We are compelled to pass beyond to the direct selection of economic objectives as a basis for the policy of the state." [6] In more cases dissatisfaction with the old formula has produced merely a general bias in favor of state intervention in the economy. This goes far to explain why the American liberal, to the endlessly articulated surprise of political philosophers, has so often turned up as an advocate of government control.

In fact, the pursuit of this alternative has not been carried very far. It has been carried much less far than conservatives, in their dreams, have been inclined to suppose. The most plausible alternative to competition is full public ownership of those industries where competition is ineffective. Few American liberals have even contemplated this possibility and some would indeed be worried men were they forced to do so. Few of the halfway houses of control have even been investigated and it is a fair guess that they wouldn't be approved if they were. A minimum requirement of planning, for an economy where competition is no longer assumed to regulate prices, would be systematic price regulation by the state. Few contemporary liberals would find this palatable. The same would be true of anything more and there can't be much that is less.

The truth is that much of the American liberal's advocacy of state intervention and planning is verbal. It is a massive deployment of words which conceals the fact that he is, for the nonce, peculiarly a man with no place to go. This was admirably illustrated immediately prior to World War II by the history of the Temporary National Economic Committee — the TNEC or Monopoly Committee. The TNEC

[6] Arthur R. Burns, *The Decline of Competition* (New York: McGraw-Hill Book Co., Inc., 1936), p. 529.

was established, in a mood of excitement and even of dedication, in response to the new knowledge of the extent of industrial concentration. In calling for the investigation, President Roosevelt declared: "The power of a few to manage the economic life of the Nation must be diffused among the many or be transferred to the public and its democratically responsible government. If prices are to be managed and administered, if the Nation's business is to be allotted by plan and not by competition, that power should not be vested in any private group. . . ." [7] The authorizing resolution called for " a full and complete study and investigation [of] the concentration of economic power in, and financial control over, production and distribution of goods and services." In the three years of its existence the Committee filled a record of 17,000 pages and produced numerous (and by no means unuseful) reports and monographs. In its conclusions it affirmed that American industry was very concentrated indeed. But it produced no recommendations of any consequence whatever. In one of the most bromidic apologias of our times, it declared in its final document that: "The members of the committee are not rash enough to believe that they can lay down a program which will solve the great problems that beset the world, but they are convinced that the information which this committee has assembled . . . will enable the people of America to know what must be done if human freedom is to be preserved." [8] The Committee was unable to approve of the economy it found but, equally, it was unable to embrace any alternative. It abandoned its task in a miasma of words. Other liberals have employed the same escape.

[7] Message of April 29, 1938. Quoted in *Monopoly and Free Enterprise* by George W. Stocking and Myron W. Watkins (New York: The Twentieth Century Fund, 1951), p. 52.

[8] *Final Report and Recommendations.* T.N.E.C. Document 35 (Washington: U.S. Government Printing Office, 1941).

There remains the possibility that within the structure of the market shared by a few firms there are practical restraints on economic power — that there is an attenuated but still workable competition which minimizes the scope for exercise of private market power and which frequently makes this structure preferable to any available alternative. In particular this line of argument has emphasized results. A market is workably competitive if, among other things, there is "a progressive technology, the passing on to consumers of the results of this progressiveness in the form of lower prices, larger output, improved prices. . . . " [9]

This pragmatic concern with results is healthy; it has usefully tempered the pessimism which followed in the wake of the new market theory. The notion of workable competition takes cognizance of the sadly overlooked point that overall consequences, which in theory are deplorable, are often in real life quite agreeable. The difficulty with the notion is that its authors have failed to make clear why what is unworkable in principle becomes workable in practice. This failure, as I shall show presently, lies in the preoccupation with competition. In the competitive model the restraint on the power of any producer was provided by the competition of other producers — it came from the same side of the market. The tendency of any seller to exploit his customers was checked, not by the customers, but by another seller across the street and by many others in the same market. It was natural that in looking for restraints on the behavior of the large seller, who was one among a few in the market, the search would be

---

[9] Edward S. Mason in "The Antitrust Laws: A Symposium," ed. by Dexter M. Keezer, *American Economic Review*, June 1949, p. 713. Professor Mason is the leading exponent of the idea of a workable competition. The notion itself owes much to the originality of Professor J. M. Clark ("Toward a Concept of Workable Competition," *American Economic Review*, June 1940).

made in the same place. Competition, even though it might be different in kind from that of the competitive model, was still the object of the search. Indeed it was assumed that competition was the only possible restraint on private market power. This preoccupation with competition kept the investigators from seeing the actual restraints on market power — those that made not competition but the economy workable.

III

At first glance the position of the businessman — the head of the large corporation in particular — would appear to have been considerably strengthened by the new shape which the problem of market power had taken. Even though the businessman's market power had come into full view, those who were alarmed were hopelessly divided. Some, accepting the logic of their own analysis, sought a reform of the whole structure of modern corporate enterprise — its disintegration into many small units. This could almost certainly come to nothing. Others were disposed to talk (or muse) about public regulation which they did not define and of which they would almost certainly be alarmed if they did. Meanwhile the businessman could remain undisturbed. He could continue to exercise a measure of power in the economy which, given our attitudes toward such authority however fulsomely they are disavowed, cannot be supposed to be unpleasant.

In his more philosophical moods, the businessman might even take a benign view of those who were moved to advocate stronger enforcement of the antitrust laws. Without doubt these laws have performed a notable role in American life as a kind of lightning rod for dissent. Whenever he feels dissatisfied with things as they are, or whenever he is stuck for a program to deal with something he believes to be wrong, the American radical has an unfailing formula. That is to demand that the antitrust laws be more rigorously enforced. For many they have had the standing of a universal cure; in 1947 they were even solemnly invoked as a device for keeping down prices and preventing inflation. No fundamental change in the American economy could or is likely to result from these demands for antitrust enforcement. Thus the businessman has no reason to be alarmed, while the dissident can feel that he has offered a bold and stalwart program. Had the antitrust laws not been available, and had dissent, accordingly, taken other forms in the past, or were it to do so in the future, the challenge might be formidable.

In practice, matters are a good deal more complicated. The head of the large corporation cannot concede that either he or his firm are possessors of any significant economic power. This is partly a matter of tradition. The competitive model made the firm and its head the automatons of market forces; it is natural that all should stick to the familiar defense. Moreover, any admission by the businessman himself that he has substantial economic power is certain to have uncomfortable consequences. Given the conviction that no man has the right to any control over the prices, wages, wealth or income of a fellow citizen, to admit possession of power is to concede guilt. For any one businessman to make such a concession is to invite the attention of the public and perhaps of the Department of Justice to his firm as a special case.

The head of the large corporation cannot even argue, as he might with logic, that he exercises authority not from choice but from necessity — that, given his size and share of the market, he cannot divest himself at will of responsibility. So to argue is to concede the justifiability of some sort of public regulation or review of his stewardship. It does not help to assert that he uses his power wisely; this is also a concession that the public interest is paramount. The businessman cannot claim that he is the natural arbiter and protector of that interest. Historians have had much sport with the immortal declaration of George F. Baer of the Reading Railroad in 1902 that "the rights and interests of the laboring man will be protected and cared for . . . by the Christian men to whom God in His infinite wisdom has given the control of the property interests of the country. . . . " Wiser men since have found the classical defense that they are but cogs in a system that accords them no power less dramatic but far safer.

Yet the new ideas contradict flatly the businessman's disavowal of his power. And the ideas are confirmed by everyday decisions of the businessman which are in conflict with his old defense. Having explained that he is governed by the market, the businessman must then decide for or against an increase in the price of steel, whether to proceed with a new mill in New England or on the Delaware and whether to stand or surrender on the question of wages and pensions. These decisions are important to the income and welfare of many; they cannot be concealed from a community that has come to look for them.

The businessman's disavowal of power also leaves him in an ambiguous position in relation to the same antitrust laws. He cannot deny the utter consistency of these laws with the doctrine by which he defends himself. Competition theoretically prevents him from exercising any important market power and permits him to have the power he has. It is obvious that he cannot oppose measures designed to enforce and strengthen competition.

But the power he does wield — the decisions he does and

must take — make him vulnerable to prosecution under the antitrust laws. He must think of the effect of his actions on the industry as a whole, which is how a monopolist thinks. This can easily carry him, by his own acts or those of subordinates, beyond the law. As the antitrust laws are now financed and enforced, the head of any large American corporation must count on the possibility of being hailed into court at least once in his lifetime. There he will face the abhorrent charge of having broken the very rules by which he defends himself and the system. He will stand exposed as a traitor to the basic doctrines of American capitalism. This is not pleasant. Virtually his only defense to the public is that the Department of Justice has made another nasty mistake. A careful reader of annual reports will learn how frequently this contention must be employed. Far more than the penalties or the costs of litigation, these ambiguities of the businessman's position explain why antitrust prosecution has its peculiar standing as a nightmare. This is not another invitation to tears for the hapless free enterpriser; in our society he is paid to worry. Nonetheless, like the liberal, the businessman could do with a new and more plausible rationalization of economic power.

CHAPTER VI

The Depression Psychosis

THE PROBLEMS of the American economy and polity just discussed have been mostly in the realm of ideas. They would have been a cause of uncertainty and insecurity even had they drawn little reinforcement from everyday experience. But to be a considerable source of alarm they needed the catalysis of experience — an experience which would force a large number of individual citizens to question the efficacy and stability of American capitalism. That experience, in a highly compelling form, was provided by the Great Depression.

The competitive model of a capitalist economy allowed, as noted, for rhythmic increases and decreases in prices and production and even for occasional bouts of unemployment. It did not contemplate the possibility of a catastrophic and enduring depression. Economists, and through them, politicians, businessmen and the public, were insulated from the need to think of such a tragedy by the benign theorem that the act of production provided the purchasing power for all that was produced at approximate full employment.

Until 1930 a *really* serious depression was not part of the experience of Americans. In late 1920 and early 1921 there was a sharp fall in prices and incomes, and, in somewhat lesser degree, in employment. But the recovery was prompt. Moreover, the whole episode was inextricably associated with the war and its aftermath and could be blamed on what economists are pleased to call exogenous forces. Except by farmers, who continued to feel themselves at a disadvantage, it was almost universally dismissed as the inevitable reaction to the wartime inflation in prices and profits.

One can only suppose that in 1929 the fates undertook, after great deliberation, to shake the confidence of the people of the United States in their economy. Nothing could have been more ingeniously or more elaborately designed to achieve this result. There was the shock effect — the sudden dramatic collapse in stock-market values with which the lives and fortunes of thousands of innocents, who only then became aware of their innocence, had become entwined. This was followed by the inexorable decline in output, values and employment which, in a little more than two years, cut the value of national production almost in half and left twelve million workers — ten and a half million more than in 1929 — without jobs and mostly without reliable means of support. Those who still had jobs lived in the penetrating fear that their turn would be next. Meanwhile hundreds of thousands of well-to-do citizens either made a sudden and irretrievable descent into poverty or dwelt in the cold fear that they soon would. It would have added to the security of the country if businessmen and bankers had escaped the debacle. But their well-publicized plight suggested, all too plainly, that they too had no formula for contending with capitalism when the latter was on shipwreck tack. The broken banker was as commonplace a figure in the news as the unemployed worker, and a much less reassuring one. The economy was the impartial destroyer of all.

When there was nothing else to hope for, it could still be hoped that the depression would be temporary. A rhythm of good times and bad was the minimum promise of the competitive model. To this shaky standard the defenders of the system repaired in droves. Then, the most malicious act of all, the depression was made to last ten years. The very notion that depressions in the United States were self-correcting — that there were corners that would be turned — became a national jest. As if to sharpen the point, a modest recovery prior to the summer of 1937, which however had left between seven and eight million still unemployed, was followed by a slump in production that was even sharper than the one following 1929. The Great Depression of the thirties never came to an end. It merely disappeared in the great mobilization of the forties. For a whole generation it became the normal aspect of peacetime life in the United States — the thing to be both feared and expected.

Ten years have now elapsed since the end of the Great Depression, five taken up by the excitements of war, five more of the greatest prosperity Americans have ever experienced. Measured by its continuing imprint on actions and attitudes, the depression clearly stands with the Civil War as one of the two most important events since the Revolution. For the great majority of Americans World War II, by contrast, was an almost casual and pleasant experience. Several million found jobs who had doubted whether they might ever find jobs again. Hundreds of thousands of others escaped the routines of middle-class employments, their boredom with which they had concealed even from themselves. Men and women who had never supposed that society would entrust them with responsibility found themselves discharging important tasks with a competence of which they alone had been previously aware. Only a minority experienced the nagging homesickness, the fear, the physical suffering and the mutilation and death which is the less pleasant destiny of the fighting soldier in wartime. Because they were a minority the war left no lasting imprint. The depression which afflicted a great majority of the people clearly did.

The depression psychosis not only contributed deeply to

the uncertainty and insecurity of Americans in the years following World War II, it also deeply influenced economic
behavior. Although the fear has been dulled somewhat by
the years of prosperity since the war and more such years
would dull it more, it is still important. The convention, so
scrupulously observed by businessmen, which bans the public
expression of any fear of economic collapse, lest to express
the fear is to invite the fact, has concealed much of this
alarm. Yet, as I have earlier suggested, nearly every major
business enterprise in the United States has been operated in
the last five years in the expectation that sooner or later there
would be a major slump. In late 1946, some 15,000 leading
business executives were asked by *Fortune* Magazine if they
expected an "extended major depression with large-scale
unemployment in the next ten years." Fifty-eight per cent of
those replying (in confidence) said they did. Of the re-
remainder, only twenty-eight per cent said no.[1] Organized
labor's preoccupation with measures to maintain employment
and the farmers' preoccupation with support prices have both
reflected the search for shelter from depression. During the
last fifteen years, the American radical has ceased to talk
about inequality or exploitation under capitalism or even its
"inherent contradictions." He has stressed, instead, the un-
reliability of its performance.

II

By the mid-thirties, the layman — whether worker, businessman, farmer or unemployed — had undoubtedly reached his
own conclusions concerning American capitalism. Asked
were its norm an equilibrium of stable prices and full employment, the conclusion of the competitive model, he would
have recommended his interrogator to the care of a good

[1] *Fortune*, February 1947, p. 34. The rest declined to say.

doctor. But, as ideas to be influential need the support of experience, so experience needs interpretation by ideas. Only then does it become the basis for generalization — for a theory. The Great Depression might, conceivably, have remained the great accident if ideas had not again intervened. These, in their mature form, made depression, or its counterpart inflation, the normal behavior pattern of uninhibited and unmanaged capitalism. While this discouraging analysis carried with it a remedy — a remedy that was received with profound enthusiasm by many economists and much of the public at large — the remedy was unorthodox and disturbing. It is only partial comfort for a patient, who is being told he is chronically ill, to learn that there are violent and painful cures for his disease.

The ideas which interpreted the depression, and which warned that depression or inflation might be as much a part of the free-enterprise destiny as stable full employment, were those of John Maynard Keynes. A case could easily be made by those who make such cases, that his were the most influential social ideas of the first half of the century. A proper distribution of emphasis as between the role of ideas and the role of action might attribute more influence on modern economic history to Keynes than to Roosevelt. Certainly his final book, *The General Theory of Employment, Interest and Money*,[2] shaped the course of events as only the books of three earlier economists — Smith's *Wealth of Nations*, Ricardo's *Principles of Political Economy* and Marx's *Capital* — have done.

This is a judgment which has the impressive support of Keynes himself. Writing to George Bernard Shaw in early 1935, he said " . . . I believe myself to be writing a book on

[2] New York: Harcourt, Brace and Co., 1936. Many of the recommendations for public action which emerge from this volume had previously been made by Keynes. However, the general acceptance of Keynes' program awaited the full development of the underlying *rationale*.

economic theory which will largely revolutionise — not, I suppose, at once but in the course of the next ten years — the way the world thinks about economic problems." [3] It is not a judgment which greater historical perspective has yet altered.

Keynes' *General Theory* could not normally be read, even by the intelligent layman, unless he was schooled in the language and, even more, in the abstractions of economics. As a result its influence on practical affairs was almost entirely by proxy. It was not from Keynes but from his interpreters at first, second or third remove that most men learned of his ideas. Millions came to accept Keynes' conclusions who had never read a word he had written. More interesting, thousands came to be advocates of his proposals who, if asked, would have indignantly denied they were Keynesians. While everyone knows that Keynes was important and influential there is still a remarkable uncertainty as to just how or why.

The major conclusion of Keynes' argument — the one of greatest general importance and the one that is relevant here — is that depression and unemployment are in no sense abnormal. (Neither, although the point is made less explicitly, is inflation.) On the contrary, the economy can find its equilibrium at any level of performance. The chance that production in the United States will be at that level where all, or nearly all, willing workers can find jobs is no greater than the chance that four, six, eight or ten million workers will be unemployed. Alternatively the demand for goods may exceed what the economy can supply even when everyone is employed. Accordingly there can be, even under peacetime conditions, a persistent upward pressure on prices, i.e., more or less serious inflation.

[3] R. F. Harrod, *The Life of John Maynard Keynes* (New York: Harcourt, Brace and Co., 1951), p. 462.

This is not the place to restate Keynes' system. However, some essentials are necessary for the more constructive tasks of this book which begin with the next chapter. Keynes destroyed and pretty much without trace, the conclusions that had been derived from Say's Law. The contention that production provided the purchasing power to buy whatever was produced meant that any given level of output was approximately stable. There could be no sudden reduction of output in response to a disappearance of purchasing power.

Output was not completely stable, for, if there happened to be unemployment at the moment, those without work could always make it worth the while of some employer somewhere to hire them by offering to work for less than the going wage. Given the competition of the competitive model, such reductions in wages could occur; the resulting reductions in costs and prices would, it was assumed, lead to an expansion of sales and an increase in employment to a point where all willing workers had jobs.[4] Thus the equilib-

[4] A slightly more technical comment seems called for here. A wage reduction can be of two sorts. It can be confined to those workers who were previously unemployed and who get work by lowering their wage demands. Wages of those already employed remain unaffected. This, of course, is to suppose that the labor market is less than perfect but given this supposition, the effect of these marginal wage reductions in increasing employment is clear. There is no reduction in the general spending in the economy such as would accompany general wage reductions. It is worth the while of employers to add the new, lower-paid workers and their income provides the wherewithal to buy what they add to production. Something very like this happened in the farm-labor market during the depression and helps explain the continuing full employment in that industry in those years. If it is assumed that the lower wages of the marginal workers bring down all wages, the employment effect is more roundabout. However, if all of the assumptions of the competitive model are rigidly respected, the result is not greatly less certain. Prices will be promptly adjusted to the lower costs; not all of the income flow will be affected by the wage reduction. There will be some substitution of labor for capital. Interest rates will fall, reducing saving. The aggregate effect will be that a somewhat smaller income than before will purchase a larger volume of goods produced (per unit) with more labor. The effect will be higher employment.

rium of the economy tended to be stable at full employment.

The act of producing and selling a product does, undeniably, place a revenue equivalent to the total value of the article produced in *someone's hands*. The eighteen hundred dollars that is spent on an automobile does re-emerge as revenue to someone whether in the form of wages, corporate or dealer profits, dividends, salesmen's commissions, repaid debt or revenues to a steel mill to be divided in turn. It is open to the receiver of this revenue either to spend it or not to spend it. That part which he spends obviously presents no problem. It is spent. It goes back into the market to buy what is produced and so far Say is vindicated.

A failure in ultimate spending must, by definition, arise in that part of the revenue from production which is saved. In the competitive model this was taken care of by the interest rate. On the interest rate was shouldered the heavy task of equating what men were willing to save with what others foresaw they could earn from borrowing and investing such savings. Were savings large and the prospects for returns from new capital investment none too favorable, the rate of interest would fall. This would discourage savers and encourage investors. The smaller volume of savings would be spent for more houses, hydroelectric plants, machine tools and other investment goods. There would be no loss of purchasing power as the result of the saving.

For many years prior to the appearance of Keynes' *General Theory*, this view of the rate of interest and of its equilibrating function had something of the standing among economists of a folk tale. It had been effectively attacked especially by Continental economists. Though it was told to the young and handed on from one generation to the next it would have been hard to find any reputable economist who would admit to believing it completely. There was a general reluctance, even, to expound it in print — Keynes once complained that he could find no full statement of the doctrine which he was attacking.[5] Yet the conclusion that savings were either invested or otherwise offset which followed from the theory was largely unchallenged. Keynes provided a theory of interest which did not depend on the supply and demand for savings. It was based, instead, on the public's desire to hold money — what he termed its liquidity preference — as against its desire for other and less liquid interest-bearing assets. It is not, in all respects, a plausible alternative but this was not important. In arguing for his alternative he succeeded, where others had failed, in persuading men of the implausibility of the older view of interest, saving and investment.

The attack on that doctrine — on the marriage of the supply of savings to the amount of investment by way of the interest rate — was what destroyed the old faith in a full-employment equilibrium. If an increase in saving, or more precisely in efforts to save, brings no fall in the interest rate there is no reason to expect that a responding expansion of investment will mop up the extra saving. An increase in investment could only be in response to a decrease in the interest rate; with the connection between savings and the interest rate broken, interest rates need no longer change with changes in the volume of saving. As a result, an increase in savings could result in a shortage of purchasing power for buying the volume of goods currently being produced. In that case the volume of goods would not continue to be produced. Production and prices would fall; unemployment would increase. This would reduce both savings and spending for current consumption with the probability that, eventually, it would reduce savings the most. At some point such

[5] R. F. Harrod, *op. cit.*, p. 453.

a reduction in total output, with its more than proportionate reduction in savings, would bring savings efforts into balance with investment intentions — despite the fact that investment would probably also have declined meanwhile.[6] This balance could be at a low level of output and income. Unemployment could be high. And this equilibrium with extensive unemployment might be quite stable.

In principle the unemployed man could still find someone to hire him by reducing his wage — and as a practical matter hundreds of thousands of urban workers retreated to agriculture during the depression where they found employment or self-employment by this formula. But there is good reason to question the practicability of such a remedy in an economy which has so far departed from the rigors of the competitive model as to have unions and common wage scales for similar work and workers. Where these exist the individual worker cannot agree, as an individual, to work for less than the going or union rate. There can, of course, be a general wage cut. In the competitive model the lower costs that would result from such a reduction would bring a prompt response in the form of efforts to increase production. This would as promptly bring down prices. Such an adjustment cannot be assumed in markets characterized by oligopoly — markets where prices are administered by a few large sellers.[7] Thus, in the modern economy, it is at least possible that the loss of purchasing power, resulting from the lower wages for the group, will be greater than the increase

[6] Thus between 1929 and 1932 the annual volume of investment in the United States (total gross private domestic investment) fell from $15.8 billion to $900 million. However, savings of individuals (not corporations) declined from $3.7 billion to — $1.4 billion. (Estimates from *The Economic Report of the President*, Council of Economic Advisers, January 1950.)

[7] This is not, strictly speaking, an argument used by Keynes. He had, in fact, a tendency to assume whatever competitive structure best served the purposes of his argument at any given point.

in total income resulting from the greater production at the lower costs. With the old explanation as to why depressions could not occur went the faith in the old remedies for the depressions that did, nonetheless, occur.

For purpose of displaying the essentials of the Keynesian argument it is convenient to assume an increase in saving and to see what happens — or rather what does not happen. The important consequence is that investment does not necessarily increase in order to absorb the saving; instead total production and employment may be reduced sufficiently to bring reduced saving into line with investment. In practice, economists have almost uniformly stressed fluctuations in investment rather than changes in saving as the important factor affecting total production. What people will endeavor to save from any given volume of income is commonly supposed to be less subject to change than what business concerns may seek to invest. It has become customary, therefore, to think of changes in investment as the principal cause of changes in total production and employment. Insufficient investment has become the shorthand Keynesian explanation of low production and high unemployment. The obvious remedy is more investment and, in principle, it is not important whether this be from private or public funds. But the expenditure of public funds is subject to central determination by government, as that of private funds is not, so the Keynesian remedy leads directly to public expenditure as a depression remedy.

It is apparent that public spending is only one of the remedies implicit in the Keynesian system. Abatement of taxes in order to leave private individuals more money to spend and measures to stimulate private investment or discourage saving would have a similar effect. However, it is always for his prodigality that a man is known — Henry

VIII for his wives, Louis XV for his mistresses and General Douglas MacArthur for his prose. The Keynesian has become forever associated with public spending.

In principle the Keynesian system is symmetrical. Set against deflation and unemployment is the equal and opposite danger of inflation. Those who make investment decisions may seek to invest more than the community saves even from the incomes which are enjoyed at full employment. A higher interest rate by Keynes' argument does not act to encourage saving — to cause people to cut down on their current consumption and thus make room for investment. If those who control investment decisions are trying to acquire more labor, materials and other resources than are being spared by savings from current consumption — and if production can no longer be readily expanded because the labor force is fully employed — it is obvious that something must happen. What happens is that prices will go up and people who had no intention of cutting down on consumption — foregoing an automobile in order that the steel could be used for a pipeline — find themselves forced to do so because of the advance in prices.

In practice, the Keynesian system was never really accepted as symmetrical. The depression psychosis afflicted economists no less than others. Although the point has been loosely and erroneously made that Keynes was "a depression economist" it is true that it was in relation to depression that his ideas were most eagerly explored. I shall have occasion to argue later that had there been equally serious discussion of their bearing on inflation — in a world where large corporations exercise measurable control over their prices and bargain with large unions — the Keynesian remedies would not have been found entirely reassuring. However, this must remain for a later chapter.

III

Keynes' impact on the economics of the English-speaking world was prompt and profound. An extension of his central point — that changes in total production and employment are an inherent part of the process by which the economy adjusts itself to movements in investment and savings and that, accordingly, neither depression nor inflation are abnormal — is now widely agreed. Some of the more detailed parts of his argument have been accepted even by those who, initially, most vigorously resisted his ideas. Indeed the protagonist whom Keynes used, somewhat unfairly, as the symbol of all he was attacking in the old system of economics, Professor Pigou of Cambridge University, came eventually to accept much of Keynes and to acknowledge most handsomely his debt.[8] Keynes' system also provided a firm theoretical basis for the statistical measurement of overall economic behavior — for the national accounting which measures the level, content and changes in total national product — which is now universally employed.[9]

At the outbreak of World War II the new system of national accounting, now generally familiar through its summary figure of Gross National Product, had just come into use in the United States, the United Kingdom and Canada. It proved indispensable for the guidance of a modern mobilization policy. It had not yet fully penetrated Germany. Partly because they were less clear than the democracies about what they were producing, how they were dividing it between military and civilian use, how they were allocat-

[8] A. C. Pigou, *Keynes' General Theory: A Retrospect* (London: Macmillan Co., 1950).

[9] Its principal American inventor was Professor Simon Kuznets of the University of Pennsylvania, for whose magnificently conceived statistical measurement Keynes, in effect, provided the underlying theory.

ing resources between immediate use and investment and how the corresponding income was being divided — all information that was displayed by the new accounts — the Germans mobilized their economic resources with considerably less skill and boldness than did England or the United States. Because they are modest men, economists never advertised the power of the weapon they had placed in the hands of their governments although its bearing on victory was considerably greater than that of atomic energy. Perhaps they were wise. Had their wartime significance been fully appreciated, some aggressive patriot would almost certainly have demanded that national income, gross national product, their components and the manner of their calculation all be made subject to strict security.

IV

The time has now come to consider the political consequences of Keynes for, more than any man of the century, he reformulated attitudes on the agitated question of the relation of the state to the economy.

The United States, in the thirties, was urgently in need of a new theory of the relation of government to economic life. The American political parties had long been in the habit of assuming full responsibility for economic well-being and of campaigning with promises of prosperity for all. The inconsistency of these promises, which Republicans and Democrats had made with equal fervor, with the role assigned to the state by the competitive model was untroublesome so long as there was reasonable prosperity in any event. It was bound to be troublesome to a party which was forced to contend with a serious depression. The New Deal came to power on the usual promises and with little clearer view than predecessor administrations of how the government might intervene to bring prosperity.

It was inevitable that the attention of liberals in a liberal administration would be directed toward the structure of the economy. The preconceptions of the competitive model guided their thinking in this direction. Implicit in the rise of big business was the possibility that it had created a structure that departed so far from the competitive model that it could not work. Two courses of action were open. The incentives which, under the competitive model, were presumed to guide businessmen to a socially desirable behavior could be replaced by some kind of central determination which would get the desired results. Perhaps businessmen could be brought together under the aegis of government and be told, or made, to agree to increase employment and stabilize wages and prices. Or, alternatively, perhaps private incentives could be rehabilitated by remaking business enterprise so that it conformed more closely to the preconceptions of the model.

Both enterprises involved the most serious difficulties. The first, which was given a trial run in the NRA, suffered from a grievous unclarity of both methods and goals. The self-interest of the businessman dictated the particular low level of employment he was offering and investment he was making in 1933. This simple fact was not altered by bringing him together with other businessmen under the supervision of a Code Authority. It seems improbable that much would have been accomplished had he been ordered directly by government to increase employment and investment outlays at his own cost and against his own assessment of interest.

To remake the economy in accordance with the requirements of the competitive model was obviously a time-consuming enterprise. To take time out to break up large corporate units and re-establish the competition of the model was hardly in keeping with the temper of a country which found depression tiresome and which was not noted for its patience. To the extent that it was contemplated in the later years of the New Deal it was as a decidedly long-run reform. There remained in 1933 only possibility of abandoning capitalism entirely. This was a project which raised the question of alternatives concerning which only a handful of Communists were in any way clear. It is hardly surprising that the early days of the New Deal were distinguished in American history for their foggy semanticism — for meaningless or incomprehensible talk about social planning, guided capitalism and industrial self-government. When stumped by a problem the American liberal rarely admits defeat. He takes the offensive with words.

It was Keynes who provided the escape from the dilemma — and the words. It would be hard, at first glance, to imagine a formula that was better designed for the American scene. The depression was the overwhelmingly important problem. The notion of an excess of savings or a deficiency of investment [10] defined the nature of the government intervention. By public borrowing or expenditure, or the appropriate changes in taxation, the government could make up for the deficiency in private spending. By so doing it could return the economy to full employment and keep it there. To the naked eye, the scope of private business decision remained as before. General Motors still decided what cars to produce, what prices to charge, how to advertise and sell them, when to build a new assembly plant and how many workers to

[10] More awkwardly but more accurately, of efforts to save and intentions to invest. By frustrating these efforts and intentions, changes in total output keep savings and investment as Keynes defines them always equal.

employ. It merely sold more cars because employees on public works projects became customers for secondhand Chevrolets, their foremen for new ones and the contractor for a Buick.

The government had always taxed: to reduce taxes and so release income for spending or, perhaps, to adjust taxes to fall more heavily on income that was likely to end up as redundant saving involved no radical departure. The government had always spent. To spend for the express purpose of absorbing savings and raising the level of output and employment in the economy, if novel, was far from revolutionary. The government borrowed for at least part of this expenditure. But the debt so created was the counterpart of private debt that would have been created had private investment absorbed the excess of savings. In any case one strong wing of Keynesian thought assumed (and still does) that periods of unemployment and of inflation would alternate at convenient intervals. Since the formula for periods of inflation seemed to be the simple obverse of that for unemployment — higher taxes, especially on income to be spent, diminished public spending and a budget surplus — the debts of one period would be liquidated by the excess revenues of the next.

V

Liberals almost spontaneously adopted the Keynesian formula. They were also puzzled by the reluctance of conservatives, especially businessmen, to embrace it. Here was protection from the overwhelming threat of depression — the only threat of potentially revolutionary proportions seemingly faced by capitalism. The businessman remained undisturbed in his prerogatives as an owner and manager and had the promise of better business to boot. What could he lose?

With time there has been some explicit and a great deal of implicit acceptance of the Keynesian formula by American businessmen. This is something to which I shall return. However, among others it encountered the sharp cleavage which exists in our attitude toward technological and social change. If a man seeks to design a better mousetrap he is the soul of enterprise; if he seeks to design a better society he is a crackpot. For those who mistrust social change it is not an argument that profits might be increased, even that disaster might be avoided. They are opposed to change and they cannot be bought. They are men of principle.

There were also more positive grounds for business opposition to Keynes than liberals have been inclined to suppose. The Keynesian system, though it implied a decidedly nonrevolutionary change in the relation of the government to the economy, implied, nonetheless, an important one. For a doctrine that excluded government it substituted one that made government indispensable. Keynes was sufficiently unpalatable when he made depression and inflation, not adventitious or war-induced misfortunes, but normal occurrences. He went on to make government the indispensable partner of business. In failing to recognize the prestige that goes with power and decision-making in American life, American liberals failed to recognize that, for some businessmen, the Keynesian remedy was at least as damaging as the depression it presumed to eliminate. Even though the businessman might profit in a narrow pecuniary sense from the new role of government there was no chance that his prestige would survive intact. Where, in economic life, people had previously looked upon business decisions as the ones that had shaped their destiny, now they would have regard for government decisions as well. Those of an Assistant Secretary of the Treasury on interest rates were now of more importance than those of any banker. Those of a regional administrator of public works on investment attained a significance greater than those of a corporation president. To share the prestige of decision-making is to lose prestige. The Keynesian remedies thus represented an assault on a valued possession. Those who were losers could hardly be expected to embrace the ideas that brought this loss. Much of their dissatisfaction was expressed in personal terms — it was directed against the Administration and against the public servants who implemented the new ideas. But a good deal was directed at Keynes. His American followers, taking at face value our conventional disavowal of any interest in power, failed to understand the discontent over its impairment.

The Keynesian system also, though unobtrusively, opened the way for a large expansion of government services and activities. This was the result of a new and very important concept of social waste which followed in its train. If the normal tendency of the economy is toward full employment, then the use of labor and other economic resources by government is at the expense of their use by the private economy. Dams and post offices are built at the cost of private consumption or investment. If there is full employment in the first place, something must be given up. But if unemployment is chronic, the dams and post offices require no sacrifice of private production or consumption. The labor, plant and materials that are used would otherwise have been unemployed. They are wasted if someone does not employ them. Again ideas had produced a topsy-turvy world! Government spending, long the mark of profligacy, was now sanctioned in the sacred name of avoiding waste. It was inevitable also that wild men would draw from this paradox, and the substantial truths on which it is built, a sanction for any and all expenditures at any and all times. Here was further discomfort for the conservative.

The Keynesian ideas had other new, heterodox and even threatening corollaries. Thrift, an ancient and once an absolute virtue, was brought into question; it suffered from the guilt of association with redundant saving and depression. A doctrine which cast doubt on so conventional a good was bound to be suspect. We Americans bring a deep theological conviction to the defense of our chosen principles. Those who dissent are not wrong, they are evil. Nothing could better prove that a man was secretly in the service of the devil or communism than that he should raise his voice against thrift.

Finally the new doctrine raised uncomfortable questions concerning both income distribution and profits. Say's Law provided a highly satisfactory defense of incomes and profits even when these were generous. They might not be deserved but, since they were either spent or saved and promptly invested, they did not impair the functioning of the economy. On the contrary they benefited it. The pressure to consume is least urgent on high personal incomes and high profits; there is the greatest chance of saving from such income and, when invested, this provides the factories, machinery, utilities and motive power by which future production is increased.

Once saving and the certainty of its utilization in investment became suspect, this defense of high personal incomes and high profits dissolved. More than that, such income became subject to a new attack. If these were the incomes whence the most saving came, it was by these that depressions were caused. By leveling off high incomes and profits one could reduce the amount of savings that had to be offset by investment at full employment. This would promote economic stability.

In the years from 1946 to 1950 profits of American business were spectacularly high — for all private corporations they ranged, after taxes, from just under $14 billion in 1946 to just under $22 billion in 1950. In 1939 they were $5 billion; in 1929 $8.4 billion.[11] The question of the fairness of these profits and the resulting personal incomes — the question of whether someone was getting more than he deserved — was hardly raised. This was the ancient objection to high profits but it is so no longer. Envy in our time is confined to the contemplation of others of nearly equal income. The postwar attack on profits, as avowed, was almost exclusively on their alleged contribution to instability. It was widely asserted that high profits were the feature of the boom which, if uncurbed, would cause the bust. This also was the handiwork of Keynes.

The disagreements arising out of Keynes' proposals should not be magnified. He was not a divisive figure; on the contrary his work was solidly in the Anglo-American tradition of compromise which seeks progress by reconciling the maximum number of conflicts of interest. But it is also easy to see how his formula, and the speed with which it was accepted, provided its own ground for uneasiness.

Enough has now been said of the sources of the insecurity of Americans of varying temper concerning their economy. The time has come to examine the substance of these doubts.

[11] *Economic Report of the President, supra.*

CHAPTER VII

The Economics of Technical Development

CLEARLY the drift of the accepted ideas concerning the economy of the United States has been toward a most dismal set of conclusions. They suggest that the economy does not work at its highest efficiency; incentives do not reward most the man who produces what people most want at least cost. The greatest reward may go to the crypto-monopolist or to the most skillful advertiser and salesman. The accepted ideas also expose a disagreeable problem of power. A plenary authority lies with the heads of private corporations, evidently also with leaders of unions, which enables them to make decisions affecting the wealth and livelihood of others. There is no reason for supposing that the economy works reliably. The depression of the thirties remains impressively on the record to suggest the possibility of serious breakdown. The accepted ideas make depression, or its counterpart inflation, as normal as good performance. True, the Keynesian system, which affirms the likelihood of such misfortune, carries with it a remedy. But it is one requiring a degree of government participation in the economy which many conservatives, to put it mildly, find repugnant.

Yet most Americans, and most foreigners whose sources of information bear a perceptible relation to the truth, undoubtedly consider the American economy, as it has performed in the last decade, a considerable success. In principle the economy pleases no one; in practice in the last ten years it has satisfied most. Social inefficiency, unrationalized power, intrusive government and depression are all matters for deep concern. But neither liberals nor conservatives, neither the rich nor all but the very poor, find the present intolerable.

Pessimism in our time is infinitely more respectable than optimism: the man who foresees peace, prosperity, and a decline in juvenile delinquency is a negligent and vacuous fellow. The man who foresees catastrophe has a gift of insight which insures that he will become a radio commentator, an editor of *Time* or go to Congress. Recognizing the risks in running counter to our national preference for gloom, it may still be worth while inquiring why the years of peace following World War II proved tolerable. Conceivably, from this analysis, one can learn how the future can be tolerable too. The task of this and the chapters following is to examine in turn the circumstances which have kept social inefficiency, private power, government intervention and unemployment from ruining us in the recent present.

II

The first reason the present is tolerable is that efficiency in the American economy appears in a deep disguise. To the man steeped in the preconceptions of the competitive model the disguise is nearly complete. The incentives in the typical American industry, the industry pre-empted by a handful of large firms, do not in fact work in the direction of maximum output at lowest prices. Subject to important restraints, which I will examine later, the market power of the individual firm is used, at any given time, to obtain prices that are higher for an output that, as a result, is smaller than would be ideal. In consumers' goods industries, great energy is, without doubt, channeled into one or another form of selling effort, which is of no perceptible benefit to the public and which is not in response to any recognizable public demand.

However, there is a major compensation for much of this inefficiency, and that is technical change. Moreover, a benign Providence who, so far, has loved us for our worries, has made the modern industry of a few large firms an almost perfect instrument for inducing technical change. It is admirably equipped for financing technical development. Its organization provides strong incentives for undertaking development and for putting it into use.[1] The competition of the competitive model, by contrast, almost completely precludes technical development.

There is no more pleasant fiction than that technical change is the product of the matchless ingenuity of the small man forced by competition to employ his wits to better his neighbor. Unhappily, it is a fiction. Technical development has long since become the preserve of the scientist and the engineer. Most of the cheap and simple inventions have, to put it bluntly, been made. Not only is development now sophisticated and costly but it must be on a sufficient scale so that successes and failures will in some measure average out. Few can afford it if they must expect all projects to pay off. This was not the case in the late eighteenth and the nineteenth century. Then, in the beginning stages of the applications of

[1] This point has been much overlooked by economists. A major exception was the late Professor Joseph A. Schumpeter in whose system the innovating role of large enterprises is strongly emphasized. See his *Capitalism, Socialism and Democracy* (New York: Harper & Bros., 2d ed., 1943), pp. 79 ff. While my analysis is in a tradition of economic theory different from his, and one of which he was frequently critical, the conclusions on this point are similar.

science and technology to industry and agriculture, there was
scope for the uncomplicated ingenuities of a Hargreaves or a
Franklin. The competition of the competitive model encouraged such ingenuity and assured the spreading of its
fruits. As elsewhere the competitive model had great appro-
priateness to the industrial society which it was designed to
interpret. Its designers were not abstruse theorists or dolts.
It is the society they interpreted that has changed.

Because development is costly, it follows that it can be
carried on only by a firm that has the resources associated
with considerable size. Moreover, unless a firm has a substantial share of the market it has no strong incentive to
undertake a large expenditure on development. There are, in
practice, very few innovations which cannot be imitated —
where secrecy or patent protection accords a considerable
advantage to the pioneer. Accordingly the competitor of the
competitive model must expect that his innovation will be
promptly copied or imitated. Whether it be a new product
or a new way of reducing the costs of producing an old one,
the change will be dispersed over a market in which he has
only an infinitely small share. The imitators, who haven't
stood the cost of development, profit along with the pioneer.
And presently prices will adjust themselves to remove entirely
the advantage of the innovator. He is thus restored to a plane
of equality with his imitators. Thus the very mechanism
which assures the quick spread of any known technology in
the purely competitive market — and which was a strong
recommendation of that market — eliminates the incentive to
technical development itself. It leaves to the pioneer, apart
from the rare case of effective patent protection, only the
fleeting rewards of a head start. Where the costs of development are considerable, there is no reason to suppose that the
returns to the pioneer will be sufficient to compensate for

the cost. On the contrary, as the costs of development in-crease — and with time and progress toward more sophisti-cated innovation they must increase — there is a diminishing likelihood that they will be recovered. The higher the level of science and technology required for change, the more nearly static an industry which conforms to the competitive model will become.

In the industry that is shared by a relatively small num-ber of large firms, the convention that excludes price com-petition does not restrain technical innovation. This remains one of the important weapons of market rivalry. The firms, typically, are large. Hence resources are available on a scale appropriate to the modern requirements of technical devel-opment. Some of them in fact are the fruits of market power — of monopoly gains. And, while imitation must be assumed and expected, the convention which limits price competition also insures that the returns, whether to a new product or from cost-reducing innovation, will accrue to the innovator as well as to its rivals for a period of time. The presence of market power makes the latter time period subject to some measure of control.

Thus, in the modern industry shared by a few large firms, size and the rewards accruing to market power combine to insure that resources for research and technical development will be available. The power that enables the firm to have some influence on prices insures that the resulting gains will not be passed on to the public by imitators (who have stood none of the costs of development) before the outlay for devel-opment can be recouped. In this way market power protects the incentive to technical development.

The net of all this is that there must be some element of monopoly in an industry if it is to be progressive. This, at first glance, is shockingly at variance with accepted notions.

Economists have long excoriated the comfortable domination of an industry by a single firm in the belief that such a
firm will sit not only on production but on progress as well.
So, far from spending money on innovation, it may even
suppress patents in order to protect existing investment in
plant and machinery.

Such a view of the behavior of a monopoly may not be
entirely in error although, as Schumpeter has argued, it may
be somewhat improbable in a world where there are always
potential substitutes and where innovation is proceeding elsewhere.[2] The error has resulted from generalizing from what
may be the plausible behavior of a single firm in possession of
the entire output of an industry to the consequences of the
monopoly power of a few firms sharing the output of an industry. Because stagnation is a plausible counterpart of monopoly in the first case it has been thought to be a likely
counterpart of the monopoly power that undoubtedly exists
in the second case. This generalization, so far from being
valid, would appear to be almost completely in error.

To be sure, some room must be left for exceptions. One
can imagine that the convention against price competition
could be extended, in the industries of small numbers, to innovation. And, as in the well-publicized instances of patent
suppression, this has undoubtedly happened. But to maintain
a convention against innovation requires a remarkably comprehensive form of collusion. This is difficult as well as
legally dangerous. While it would be going too far to say
that oligopoly insures progress, technical development is all
but certain to be one of the instruments of commercial rivalry
when the number of firms is small. Like advertising and
salesmanship — and unlike price competition which is unique
in this respect — technical development is a safe rather than

[2] *Ibid.*, pp. 101–2.

a reciprocally destructive method by which any one firm can advance itself against its few powerful rivals.

Moreover, in a community which sets great store by progress, technical progress is an important source of business prestige. An American business concern simply cannot afford the reputation of being unprogressive. If it has no laboratories it must imagine some; an annual report that makes no reference to research is unthinkable. Such an environment is highly unfavorable to any systematic restraint on innovation.

Thus there can be little doubt that oligopoly, both in theory and in fact, is strongly oriented toward change. There can be no serious doubt at all that the setting for innovation, which is so favorable in this market structure, disappears almost entirely as one approaches the competition of the competitive model.

III

These propositions can be readily verified by experience. The American farmer, the producer who most closely approaches the competitor of the model, does almost no research on his own behalf. It was the foresight of genius that caused this to be recognized at an early stage in our history, with the result that technical development within this field has been almost completely socialized. We now take for granted that technical development in agriculture as such will come from the State Experiment Stations and from the United States Department of Agriculture. Not minimizing for a moment the well-publicized efforts of the men of literature who have invested their royalties in land, there would be little technical development and not much progress in agriculture were it not for government-supported research supplemented by that

of the large corporations who devise and sell products to the
farmer. The individual farmer cannot afford a staff of
chemists to develop an animal protein factor which makes
different proteins interchangeable as feeds. So many would
appropriate the innovation so quickly, without having contributed to the cost of development, that it wouldn't profit
any farmer to try.

The other industries which are distinguished by a close
approach to the competitive model are also distinguished, one
can almost say without exception, by a near absence of research
and technical development. The bituminous coal industry,
apart from a handful of very large operators, the cotton textile industry, apart from a few very large groups of mills, the
clothing industry, the lumber industry and the shoe industry
do very little research. None of them are thought of as technically progressive industries. All of them (apart always from
the few large firms they contain and which help prove the
case) roughly meet the specifications of the competitive
model. They also conform to the ideal which the American
economist has had anciently in mind. No firm in these industries (the few special cases again excepted) has appreciable
influence on prices; each is forced by circumstances which it
cannot control to search for the greatest efficiency of operation; in most of them entry and exit are admirably free; few
of the firms in these industries engage in extensive competitive
advertising and salesmanship. Yet almost no one would select
them as a showpiece of American industrial achievement.
The showpieces are, with rare exceptions, the industries which
are dominated by a handful of large firms. The foreign visitor,
brought to the United States by the Economic Cooperation
Administration, visits the same firms as do attorneys of the
Department of Justice in their search for monopoly.

The reductions in cost, and the consequent increases in efficiency from technical change can be of a wholly different order of magnitude from those sacrificed as the result of the exercise of market power. Thus it comes about that a slight continuing loss of efficiency, as compared with ideal performance, from the possession of market power is regularly offset and more than offset by large gains from technical development. Economists, aided by the new market theory, have fixed their attention on the loss and have overlooked the offset. In concentrating on the inefficiency of the steam engine — specifically the fact that it is not being worked to ideal capacity — they have failed to notice that the owner was designing a gas turbine.

IV

A comparison of the oil with the bituminous coal industry usefully illustrates the point being emphasized. The oil industry is an unquestioned oligopoly; in any market area there are a few large firms and the characteristic fringe of independents. Over the years it has been under repeated attack for violation of the antitrust laws; it has rarely been free of suspicion of holding prices above the level that would be associated with more vigorous price competition. Profits have generally been excellent. Yet few would be inclined to trade the oil industry for the bituminous coal industry which, abstracting from the stabilization operations of John L. Lewis, approaches the competition of the model.

The oil industry is clearly progressive — almost as progressive, perhaps, as the uncommonly attractive brochures of its member companies unreluctantly concede. As the result of its enterprise in petroleum exploration and recovery, in developing new products, and in engineering new methods of transporting both petroleum and products, the consumer of gasoline and fuel oil has been a far more fortunate man than the consumer of coal. The continuing shift of customers from the admirably competitive coal industry to the dubiously competitive oil industry emphasizes the point.

It seems reasonable to suppose that if the same technical talent that has been devoted to the search for oil, or to its utilization, had been brought to bear on coal-mining in the last half-century, the coal industry would be very different from what it is today. New techniques of recovery might long since have been developed. Men would no longer toil like moles in mining operations that "under the most favorable conditions are hazardous and highly inefficient . . . an unpleasant, uninspiring and none too healthy occupation." [3] It is significant, by way of verifying the technical limitations of competition, that recent efforts to raise the technology of coal production have required the co-operative effort of the industry — some three hundred operators, railroads and equipment suppliers now jointly support Bituminous Research, Inc. — and that the significant work on the hydrogenation of coal has been under government sponsorship. One of the country's experienced research administrators has observed of the coal industry that "An industry with 6,000 little units has made a terribly difficult pattern on which to develop modern industrial research programs." [4]

---

[3] "Coal I: The Industrial Darkness," *Fortune*, March 1947. Quoted from *Industrial Engineering and Chemistry*, August 1946.

[4] Frank A. Howard, *ibid*., p. 87. It must be observed that the anthracite industry, the ownership of which is considerably more concentrated than bituminous mining, has not, at least until recent times, been credited with any strongly progressive tendencies. There appear, however, to have been special reasons, relating generally to character of ownership, for this.

v

Thus, while the incentives in the American economy do not, at any given moment, act to encourage the largest possible production at the lowest possible price, this is not the tragedy that it appears to be at first glance. The market concentration of American industry that is affirmed by the statistics and condemned by the competitive model turns out on closer examination to be favorable to technical change. To get the ideal equilibrium of price and output of the competitive model, we should almost certainly have to forego the change. Life might be simpler were we to do so, but progress, as it is called, is a wheel to which we are all bound.

In all this there is less comfort for the businessman than might appear. He must still defend himself from the charge that he is too big and that he is partially monopolistic with the reply that he is really competitive in the classical sense. In the words of a leading oil company, speaking recently of the Gulf Coast refining market, he must aver that in his industry the "truest, finest form of competitive pricing exists." [5] For competition, with us, is more than a technical concept. It is also a symbol of all that is good. Even though we mightn't survive under a regime of competition of classical purity we must still worship at its throne.

[5] *Competition Makes Gasoline Prices* (Philadelphia: Sun Oil Company, n.d.).

CHAPTER VIII

The Unseemly Economics of Opulence

THERE IS a deeply held belief, the Puritan antecedents of which are clear, that if a wealthy man admits even to himself that he can afford a measure of recklessness in his expenditures, an angry God will strike him dead — or certainly take away his money. This holds also for nations. The utmost reticence must be observed in talking about the affluence of the United States. It is permissible to concede, even with a certain amount of pride, that the United States is a wealthy country. But to conclude that in peacetime this opulence excuses a certain amount of social waste is to invite the divine fury that immolated Sodom and Gomorrah. Yet a great many things about the United States can be explained only by its wealth. Although economists have long respected the tabu on drawing conclusions from it, in the service of science certain risks must now be run.

Not even the genius of the adman has been wholly equal to the task of proving that the paper, ether and skills employed in, say, cigarette advertising are related to any urgent public need. As with cigarette advertising so, presumably, with highway billboards, redundant service stations, glossy packages, bread that is first denatured and then fortified, high-pressure salesmanship, singing commercials and the concept of the captive audience. All, in one way or another, are apparently the result of incentives which guide the energies of men not toward but away from maximum social efficiency. Few would insist that these activities are in response to any very pressing desire of the American people. This is the criterion of efficiency of the competitive model. By this standard the American economy is undoubtedly a wasteful one.

However, much of the discussion of the vast activity of selling and advertising in the American economy — that which concerns economics rather than taste — has missed the point. Economists and a good many others have pointed to the energies devoted to it with shock or alarm. Those who make their living by it have replied, both in anger and in sorrow, that it isn't wasteful at all. Some bold spirits, with a knack for generalization, have said that all critics of selling expenditure are subversive. The truth does not lie in between but elsewhere. Our proliferation of selling activity is the counterpart of comparative opulence. Much of it is inevitable with high levels of well-being. It may be waste but it is waste that exists because the community is too well off to care.

II

In a country where, as the result of maximum exertion of all, only a bare minimum of food, clothing, fuel and shelter can be provided, it would indeed be intolerable to have some firms or industries tacitly restricting production and sustaining prices. The price of such a monopoly in, say, the coal-mining industry would be an insufficiency of coal in relation to what consumers desperately need. This might be partially offset by a somewhat greater supply of food. The men and resources who, under more ideal circumstances, would be employed in the mines, would, as the result of the restriction there, find employment in agriculture. But the consequences for the insufficiently heated public would be far from ideal.

Similarly such a community could ill afford to have any considerable fraction of its labor force concocting sales slogans for its limited supply of bread, writing advertising copy for its meager stock of clothing, putting its few vegetables into cellophane packages or otherwise bringing the arts of direct salesmanship to bear on its poverty-stricken consumers. In such a land the whole force, male and female, of J. Walter Thompson, Du Pont Cellophane, and Mr. Elmo Roper should without question be at work producing potatoes, beans and coal so that people might be slightly less hungry and cold.

In fact, in such a community, this labor (perhaps after an appropriate rehabilitation for manual employments) would have no choice but to seek these utilitarian occupations. It is not necessary to advertise food to hungry people, fuel to cold people or houses to the homeless. No one could make a living doing so. The need and the opportunity to persuade people arise only as people have the income to satisfy relatively unimportant wants, of the urgency of which they are not automatically aware. The social inefficiency of a wealthy community grows with the growth in wealth that goes far to make this inefficiency inconsequential.

Thus, while the forty-two million dollars worth of skill, art and paper spent in 1949 for cigarette advertising and the twenty-nine million dollars devoted to alcoholic beverages served no urgent social purpose the same is true of the cigarettes and the liquor. It is not clear that the community would be better off if those now engaged in selling tobacco and liquor were employed instead in the production of more and cheaper cigarettes and whiskey. (Both the alcoholic and the cigarette hangover seem now to be sufficiently institutionalized.) It is not certain, always assuming peace, that Mr. James H. Blandings and the other employees of Banton and Dascomb are needed in any alternative employment — they are not needed, as all recent history shows, in the production of potatoes. The alternative use of the resources which a wealthy community appears to use frivolously will always be in other frivolous employments. It will be in the production of things of no very great consequence by any standards.

III

It will be worth while to examine a little more closely the relation of advertising and selling expenditures to a state of relatively high opulence. These expenditures are made for a variety of purposes. The department stores advertise for no more complex purpose than to let customers know what they have, what they would especially like to sell at the moment, and at what prices. The same motive lies behind an appreciable amount of consumers' goods selling in general. In one way or another the vendor has always had to cry his wares; the modern techniques that are brought to the service of this particular task may be no more costly or no more raucous than those that have been used throughout time.

This kind of salesmanship invites no comment on grounds of social efficiency. Indeed the New York housewife who was forced to do without Macy's advertising would have a sense of loss second only to that from doing without Macy's. However in a consumers' goods industry shared by a comparatively small number of sellers — the characteristic industry of the contemporary American economy — advertising and selling activity is assumed in modern economics to be undertaken for one or both of two further purposes. It may be, simply, an instrument of commercial rivalry. Price competition having been foresworn as self-destructive, the firm turns to its salesmen and advertising agency to find new customers and to win customers away from its rivals. The firm is seeking, in the economist's terms, to move its demand curve to the right. Such an effort to get more is necessary, in a world where others are doing the same, if the firm is merely to hold its own. Only the very disingenuous can suppose, or argue, that this form of selling effort is merely to make the customer aware that the firm has something to sell. Americans would indeed be mentally retarded if they still had to be advised that the American Tobacco Company has Lucky Strikes to dispose of.

It is also generally agreed that the firm may be seeking, often implicitly, through its advertising and salesmanship so to establish its own personality that it will be protected in some measure from other firms which do not reliably observe the convention against price competition. If a firm is able to persuade the public that its brand of toothpaste, pancake flour, razor blades or aspirin has qualities that are unique, or if it can merely get shoppers to name its brand without thought when they go into a store, then it is protected in some measure from the rivalry of other firms who sell the same product at a lower price. In so enhancing the market power which it has over its own brand, it acquires some freedom to move its own price without inviting loss of custom. The price cuts of other firms can be viewed with some equanimity. Economic theory has given much attention to this process of "product differentiation" in the last fifteen years. As a motive, either overt or implicit, for advertising and other selling expenditure its importance has been considerably exaggerated. Simple interfirm rivalry is almost certainly far more important. Still, it is a recognizable phenomenon and the wastes associated with efforts to build up brand monopolies have been greatly deplored.

There could be no great volume of selling expenditure of either of these sorts, except in a wealthy community. In such a community the money dispensed in any given purchase is not of high importance to the person spending it — in the language of economics, the marginal utility of money is low. In such a community, also, a great many different purchases are made by each individual. The result is that no single purchase is worth a great deal of thought; there are too many of them for each to be considered in detail. Accordingly the purchaser is a ready subject for the attentions of the advertiser and the salesman. He even allows himself to be influenced by imaginary or contrived virtues, because he is not sufficiently under the pressure of want to learn whether or not these virtues are imaginary. He yields to the influence of suggestion because he is not obliged, by want, to think about his actions. On going into a store he repeats a brand name that has been iterated and reiterated on the radio because the money he is spending is not of sufficient importance to justify his ascertaining whether there are better and cheaper alternatives. Those who are persuaded that the buyer is victimized need to realize that, in the first instance, he is the victim of his own comparative well-being.

The opportunity for product differentiation — for associating monopoly power with the brand or personality of a particular seller — is almost uniquely the result of opulence. A hungry man could never be persuaded that bread that is softened, sliced, wrapped and enriched is worth more than a cheaper and larger loaf that will fill his stomach. A southern cropper will not, as the result of advertising, develop a preference for one brand of cooked, spiced and canned ham over another. He will buy plain sidemeat. No one would

advertise the sound-effects of processed breakfast foods striking the milk to Scottish crofters who have only the resources
to buy oatmeal. In such communities all the commercial advantages lie with the producers of plain bread, sidemeat and
oatmeal.

For the same reasons, the tendency for commercial rival-
ries, in the absence of price competition, to be channeled into
advertising and salesmanship would disappear in a poor community. One cannot be certain that the convention against
price competition, itself, could be maintained. The nicotine
addict, who now automatically buys one or another of the
standard brands of cigarettes, would, under the whiplash of
necessity, become an inviting market for a cheaper product.
The firm that provided it would acquire customers with a
rush. Something very like this happened during the early years
of the depression when millions of impoverished smokers
turned enthusiastically to the ten-cent brands of cigarettes.
In any case, for maintaining the convention against price
competition, it is a great help to have customers who do not
care — even if, on occasion, they think they do.

There is a legend, with a great appeal to simple men, that
Americans are a nation of salesmen because they have some
peculiar virtuosity in this craft. There are more salesmen,
and salesmanship is more highly developed, in the United
States than elsewhere in the world. But the explanation lies
not with national character but with national wealth. The
latter means, of course, that there are more goods to be sold.
But even more, it means that psychological, not physical,
considerations control desire. The biological minimums are
covered. As a result that modern practitioner of applied
psychology, the salesman, gets his opportunity. Sent to practice on Indians or Chinese or even French peasants he would
be a dismal failure.

Many of my fellow economists will have difficulty in

sharing the equanimity with which I here view selling costs and the so-called wastes of distribution. Economics began in the eighteenth and nineteenth centuries when men were really poor. Two of its great pioneers, Malthus and Ricardo, held that grinding poverty was the fate of man — any surplus wealth, above the requirements for bare subsistence, would be promptly absorbed into the additional mouths that wealth itself would spawn. In such a society inefficiency was, indeed, an evil thing. It denied bread to the hungry and clothing to the naked even though, if these became available, they launched a new cycle of conception and birth that reestablished the common poverty. Western man, as the result of an unsuspected preference for comfort over procreation, and aided by some inexpensive appliances, has escaped from this cycle of poverty. In the United States, in recent times, for most people the biological minimums of food, clothing and even shelter have been covered as a matter of course. By comparison, the further wants are comparatively unimportant. Economists, nonetheless, have stuck firmly to their conviction that anything that denies the community additional goods or services, however casual their significance, is the greatest of sins. They have brought the mentality of nineteenth-century poverty to the analysis of twentieth-century opulence.

The result is an inefficient deployment of the economist's own resources. He is excessively preoccupied with goods *qua* goods; in his preoccupation with goods he has not paused to reflect on the relative unimportance of the goods with which he is preoccupied. He worries far too much about partially monopolized prices or excessive advertising and selling costs for tobacco, liquor, chocolates, automobiles and soap in a land which is already suffering from nicotine poisoning and alcoholism, which is nutritionally gorged with sugar, which is filling its hospitals and cemeteries with those who have been maimed or murdered on highways and which is dangerously neurotic about normal body odors.

IV

It is now time to relent slightly and make some needed overtures to orthodoxy. The purpose of the last and the present chapter has been to ascertain how, in spite of the apparent inefficiencies of the American economy, we still manage to survive. We survive partly because we have failed fully to appreciate the extraordinarily high efficiency of technical change and the extraordinarily favorable organization of the economy for inducing it and partly because social efficiency itself has been overemphasized in an economy which has escaped far above the poverty line. This is not a mandate for a total neglect of efficiency. For one thing there are still many poor people in the United States. They bear the higher prices associated with monopoly power and the higher costs of distribution along with those who can afford them and who, as the result of their escape from physical to psychological standards of consumption, actually encourage such expenditure. There are still many who would live fuller and better lives if elementary goods were produced more abundantly and more cheaply. Housing is a case in point.

Furthermore, the counterpart of monopoly power, if uncorrected by forces I shall examine in the next chapter, is an unsatisfactory allocation of labor and other resources between industries and an unnecessary inequality in the distribution of personal incomes.

The effect of monopoly power on the use of resources has classically been supposed to result in too little employment in the monopolized industries. There is some evidence that in the United States the most damaging effect is, in fact, in encouraging excessive employment in the competitive industries. This part of the economy provides special opportunities to the man who is seeking employment or to employ himself. In the competitive model he can always get employment by sufficiently lowering his wage; where there are parts of the economy, like agriculture, which still conform to the model, these offer that valued opportunity to the independent job seeker. There is a strong possibility, especially when there is less than full employment in the economy, that these industries will attract a heavy surplus of workers. By crowding into this part of the economy they lower, unduly, the returns to those already there. This has been the fate of American agriculture in the past and perhaps also of the textile, clothing and needlework trades.

In agriculture the problem has been made especially acute by a higher birth rate than in the cities which requires that there be a steady migration to the cities if any given ratio of rural to urban employment is to be maintained. During the depression years the farm-labor force grew substantially as the result of the virtual stoppage of migration to the cities and the return of those who had previously migrated. Even in more favorable times, overemployment in agriculture raises serious problems of maintaining standards of education, health and welfare at civilized levels in the regions of dense rural population.

In one way or another nearly all of the great American fortunes are based on the present or past possession of monopoly power. It is to oil, railroads, steel, copper, urban real estate that yesterday's fortunes and the higher of today's unearned incomes trace. Agriculture, bituminous-coal mining, textile and clothing manufacture have produced few men of great wealth. Income inequality, like monopoly, distorts the use of resources. It diverts them from the wants of the many to the esoteric desires of the few — if not from bread to cake at least from Chevrolets to Cadillacs. Unnecessary inequality in income — unnecessary in the sense that it does not reward differences in intelligence, application or willingness to take risks — may also impair economic stability. The saving or spending of income that accrues in large chunks to relatively few people is subject to far more erratic impulses than the saving or spending of income of wage and salary earners. Accordingly, there are good reasons for continuing to worry about social inefficiency. At the same time no one should be at loss as to why we survive it.

v

Before taking leave of the unseemly subject of opulence, one of its further consequences must be observed. There is a widely held view that the economic management of the United States is a task requiring the utmost wisdom and subtlety. As a corollary, the utmost peril is implicit in every government decision. In the last two years (as I write) brave men have shuddered at the consequences of reducing taxes (or not reducing them); of passing a public-housing bill (and of not passing it); of the perils associated with peril points in tariffs (and of the consequences of not reducing tariffs); of the ruin that awaits the dairy industry in untaxed and colored margarine and the ruin that awaits the cotton grower if discrimination against cottonseed oil continues.

The time may come when the strength of the American economy will turn on the quality of government decisions but it will be in war or under the threat of war. It has not turned on such decisions in the past. The consequences for general economic welfare of most government decisions has been imperceptible. The first reason is our nearly universal tendency to confuse close decisions with important ones. The most difficult decisions are, normally, the least important. They involve a choice between courses of action which are almost equally favorable — or, on occasion, almost equally unhappy. Different men assess the effects of the alternative courses of action differently and the very closeness of the outcome causes them to marshal their arguments elaborately. Our much-used dialectic of exaggeration is also brought liberally to bear in the argument. Infinite benefit is pictured for one course, utter disaster for another. Were the choice in fact between great good and great damage, the decision would not be debated.

The other reason that government decisions have been relatively unimportant is that we have frequently been able to choose the wrong course rather than the right one because wealth has acted as a solvent for such error. None of the real sources of well-being — the endowment of physical resources and the education and energy of the people — are ever seriously compromised by any government decision. Hence, while unwise government decisions may, in the past, have affected the rate of economic growth, it has been but rarely that one could identify their consequences. This is at least implicitly recognized. Alarm over pending actions by government on economic matters, which frequently reaches almost pathological proportions when the decision is pending, almost invariably evaporates completely once the action is taken.

Wisdom in economic policy is not to be deplored. But one of the profound sources of American strength has been the margin for error provided by our endowment. In the

United Kingdom, especially in recent times, there has been little latitude for mistakes. Government management of economic affairs has had, accordingly, to be far more precise than it has ever been with us. An Eightieth Congress occupying the House of Commons or a sizeable cadre of Missouri Democrats in Whitehall, would, on many occasions in the last two decades, have brought about a fairly prompt liquidation of what remains of the British Empire.

Wealth does more than provide a margin for error. In the United Kingdom and other Western European countries, social reform — the provision of additional income, services and security for the underprivileged — has been at the fairly direct expense of the privileged. The clash of interest between those who have and those who have not is obvious and inescapable. With the single exception of the emancipation of the slaves, no measure for the assistance of any group in the United States has brought an *identifiable* reduction in the income of any other group. The costs of free education, social security, assistance to farmers and like measures of domestic welfare have been deeply disguised by the general increase in income. (In modern times they have also been small in comparison with the far greater costs of defense and war.) Had the assessment of these costs been directly against the static incomes of those who paid but did not benefit, the debate concerning them would have been a good deal more bitter than it was. Wealth, and especially growing wealth, has not only been a solvent for mistakes. It has also been a solvent for what, in its absence, might have been grave social strains.

CHAPTER IX

The Theory of Countervailing Power

ON THE NIGHT of November 2, 1907, the elder Morgan played solitaire in his library while the panic gripped Wall Street. When the other bankers had divided up the cost of saving the tottering Trust Company of America, he presided at the signing of the agreement, authorized the purchase of the Tennessee Coal & Iron Company by the Steel Corporation to encourage the market, cleared the transaction with President Roosevelt and the panic was over. There, as legend has preserved and doubtless improved the story, was a man with power a self-respecting man could fear.

A mere two decades later, in the crash of 1929, it was evident that the Wall Street bankers were as helpless as everyone else. Their effort in the autumn of that year to check the collapse in the market is now recalled as an amusing anecdote; the heads of the New York Stock Exchange and the National City Bank fell into the toils of the law and the first went to prison; the son of the Great Morgan went to a Congressional hearing in Washington and acquired fame, not for his authority, but for his embarrassment when a circus midget was placed on his knee.

As the banker, as a symbol of economic power, passed into the shadows his place was taken by the giant industrial corporation. The substitute was much more plausible. The association of power with the banker had always depended on the somewhat tenuous belief in a "money trust" — on the notion that the means for financing the initiation and expansion of business enterprises was concentrated in the hands of a few men. The ancestry of this idea was in Marx's doctrine of finance capital; it was not susceptible to statistical or other empirical verification at least in the United States.

By contrast, the fact that a substantial proportion of all production was concentrated in the hands of a relatively small number of huge firms was readily verified. That three or four giant firms in an industry might exercise power analogous to that of a monopoly, and not different in consequences, was an idea that had the most respectable of ancestry in classical economics. So as the J. P. Morgan Company left the stage, it was replaced by the two hundred largest corporations — giant devils in company strength. Here was economic power identified by the greatest and most conservative tradition in economic theory. Here was power to control the prices the citizen paid, the wages he received, and which interposed the most formidable of obstacles of size and experience to the aspiring new firm. What more might it accomplish were it to turn its vast resources to corrupting politics and controlling access to public opinion?

Yet, as was so dramatically revealed to be the case with the omnipotence of the banker in 1929, there are considerable gaps between the myth and the fact. The comparative importance of a small number of great corporations in the American economy cannot be denied except by those who have a singular immunity to statistical evidence or striking capacity to manipulate it. In principle the American is controlled, livelihood and soul, by the large corporation; in practice he seems not to be completely enslaved. Once again the danger is in the future; the present is still tolerable. Once again there may be lessons from the present which, if learned, will save us in the future.

II

As with social efficiency, and its neglect of technical dynamics, the paradox of the unexercised power of the large corporation begins with an important oversight in the underlying economic theory. In the competitive model — the economy of many sellers each with a small share of the total market — the restraint on the private exercise of economic power was provided by other firms on the same side of the market. It was the eagerness of competitors to sell, not the complaints of buyers, that saved the latter from spoliation. It was assumed, no doubt accurately, that the nineteenth-century textile manufacturer who overcharged for his product would promptly lose his market to another manufacturer who did not. If all manufacturers found themselves in a position where they could exploit a strong demand, and mark up their prices accordingly, there would soon be an inflow of new competitors. The resulting increase in supply would bring prices and profits back to normal.

As with the seller who was tempted to use his economic power against the customer, so with the buyer who was tempted to use it against his labor or suppliers. The man who paid less than prevailing wage would lose his labor force to those who paid the worker his full (marginal) contribution to earnings. In all cases the incentive to socially desirable behavior was provided by the competitor. It was to the same side of the market and thus to competition that economists came to look for the self-regulatory mechanism of the economy.

They also came to look to competition exclusively and in formal theory still do.   The notion that there might be another regulatory mechanism in the economy has been almost completely excluded from economic thought. Thus, with the widespread disappearance of competition in its classical form and its replacement by the small group of firms if not in overt, at least in conventional or tacit collusion, it was easy to suppose that since competition had disappeared, all effective restraint on private power had disappeared. Indeed this conclusion was all but inevitable if no search was made for other restraints and so complete was the preoccupation with competition that none was made.

In fact, new restraints on private power did appear to replace competition. They were nurtured by the same process of concentration which impaired or destroyed competition. But they appeared not on the same side of the market but on the opposite side, not with competitors but with customers or suppliers. It will be convenient to have a name for this counterpart of competition and I shall call it *countervailing power*.[1]

To begin with a broad and somewhat too dogmatically stated proposition, private economic power is held in check by the countervailing power of those who are subject to it. The first begets the second. The long trend toward concentration of industrial enterprise in the hands of a relatively few firms has brought into existence not only strong sellers, as economists have supposed, but also strong buyers as they have failed to see. The two develop together, not in precise step but in such manner that there can be no doubt that the one is in response to the other.

[1] I have been tempted to coin a new word for this which would have the same convenience as the term competition and had I done so my choice would have been "countervailence." However, the phrase "countervailing power" is more descriptive and does not have the raw sound of any newly fabricated word.

The fact that a seller enjoys a measure of monopoly power, and is reaping a measure of monopoly return as a result, means that there is an inducement to those firms from whom he buys or those to whom he sells to develop the power with which they can defend themselves against exploitation. It means also that there is a reward to them, in the form of a share of the gains of their opponents' market power, if they are able to do so. In this way the existence of market power creates an incentive to the organization of another position of power that neutralizes it.

The contention I am here making is a formidable one. It comes to this: Competition which, at least since the time of Adam Smith, has been viewed as the autonomous regulator of economic activity and as the only available regulatory mechanism apart from the state, has, in fact, been superseded. Not entirely, to be sure. There are still important markets where the power of the firm as (say) a seller is checked or circumscribed by those who provide a similar or a substitute product or service. This, in the broadest sense that can be meaningful, is the meaning of competition. The role of the buyer on the other side of such markets is essentially a passive one. It consists in looking for, perhaps asking for, and responding to the best bargain. The active restraint is provided by the competitor who offers, or threatens to offer, a better bargain. By contrast, in the typical modern market of few sellers, the active restraint is provided not by competitors but from the other side of the market by strong buyers. Given the convention against price competition, it is the role of the competitor that becomes passive.

It was always one of the basic presuppositions of competition that market power exercised in its absence would invite the competitors who would eliminate such exercise of power. In other words competition was regarded as a *self-generating* regulatory force. The doubt whether this was in fact so after a market had been pre-empted by a few large sellers, after entry of new firms had become difficult and after existing firms had accepted a convention against price competition, was what destroyed the faith in competition as a regulatory mechanism. Countervailing power is also a self-generating force and this is a matter of great importance. Something, although not very much, could be claimed for the regulatory role of the strong buyer in relation to the market power of sellers, did it happen that, as an accident of economic development, such strong buyers were frequently juxtaposed to strong sellers. However it is far more important that, as with the ancient presupposition concerning competition, the regulatory role of the strong buyer, in relation to the market power of the strong seller, is also self-generating. As noted, power on one side of a market creates both the need for, and the prospect of reward to, the exercise of countervailing power from the other side.[2] In the market of small numbers, the self-generating power of competition is a chimera. That of countervailing power, by contrast, is readily assimilated to the common sense of the situation and its existence, once we have learned to look for it, is readily subject to empirical verification.

Market power can be exercised by strong buyers against

[2] This has been one of the reasons I have rejected the terminology of bilateral monopoly in characterizing this phenomenon. As bilateral monopoly is treated in economic literature, it is an adventitious occurrence. This, obviously, misses the point and it is one of the reasons that the investigations of bilateral monopoly, which one would have thought might have been an avenue to the regulatory mechanisms here isolated, have in fact been a blind alley. However, this line of investigation has also been sterilized by the confining formality of the assumptions of monopolistic and (more rarely) oligopolistic motivation and behavior with which it has been approached. (Cf. for example, Willian H. Nicholls, *Imperfect Competition within Agricultural Industries*, Ames, Iowa: 1941, pp. 58 ff.) As noted later, oligopoly facilitates the exercise of countervailing market power bv enabling the strong buyer to play one seller off against another.

weak sellers as well as by strong sellers against weak buyers. In the competitive model, competition acted as a restraint on both kinds of exercise of power. This is also the case with countervailing power. In turning to its practical manifestations, it will be convenient, in fact, to begin with a case where it is exercised by weak sellers against strong buyers.

III

The operation of countervailing power is to be seen with the greatest clarity in the labor market where it is also most fully developed. Because of his comparative immobility, the worker has long been highly vulnerable to private economic power. The customer of any particular steel mill, at the turn of the century, could always take himself elsewhere if he felt he was being overcharged. Or he could exercise his sovereign privilege of not buying steel at all. The worker had no comparable freedom if he felt he was being underpaid. Normally he could not move and he had to have work. Not often has the power of one man over another been used more callously than in the American labor market after the rise of the large corporation. As late as the early twenties, the steel industry worked a twelve-hour day and seventy-two-hour week with an incredible twenty-four-hour stint every fortnight when the shift changed.

No such power is exercised today and for the reason that its earlier exercise stimulated the counteraction that brought it to an end. In the ultimate sense it was the power of the steel industry, not the organizing abilities of John L. Lewis and Philip Murray, that brought the United Steel Workers into being. The economic power that the worker faced in the sale of his labor — the competition of many sellers deal-

ing with few buyers — made it necessary that he organize
for his own protection. There were rewards to the power
of the steel companies in which, when he had successfully
developed countervailing power, he could share.

As a general though not invariable rule there are strong
unions in the United States only where markets are served
by strong corporations. And it is not an accident that the
large automobile, steel, electrical, rubber, farm-machinery and non-ferrous metal-mining and smelting companies all
bargain with powerful CIO unions. Not only has the
strength of the corporations in these industries made it necessary for workers to develop the protection of countervailing
power, it has provided unions with the opportunity for getting something more as well. If successful they could share
in the fruits of the corporation's market power. By contrast
there is not a single union of any consequence in American
agriculture, the country's closest approach to the competitive
model. The reason lies not in the difficulties in organization;
these are considerable, but greater difficulties in organization
have been overcome. The reason is that the farmer has not
possessed any power over his labor force, and at least until
recent times has not had any rewards from market power,
which it was worth the while of a union to seek. As an interesting verification of the point, in the Great Valley of
California, the large farmers of that area have had considerable power vis-à-vis their labor force. Almost uniquely in
the United States, that region has been marked by persistent
attempts at organization by farm workers.

The other industries which are not marked by any high
degree of concentration, and accordingly are not especially
powerful in their labor market, do not normally have strong
unions. The textile industry, boot and shoe manufacture,
lumbering and other forest industries in most parts of the

country, and smaller wholesale and retail enterprises, are all
cases in point. I do not advance the theory of countervailing
power as a monolithic explanation of trade-union organization; in the case of bituminous-coal mining and the clothing
industry, for example, the unions have emerged as a supplement to the weak market position of the operators and manufacturers. They have assumed price- and market-regulating
functions that are the normal functions of management.
Nevertheless, as an explanation of the incidence of trade-
union strength in the American economy, the theory of
countervailing power clearly fits the broad contours of
experience.

IV

The labor market serves admirably to illustrate the incentives
to the development of countervailing power and it is of great
importance in this market. However, its development, in response to positions of market power, is pervasive in the economy. As a regulatory device one of its most important manifestations is in the relation of the large retailer to the firms
from which it buys. The way in which countervailing power
operates in these markets is worth examining in some detail.

One of the seemingly harmless simplifications of formal
economic theory has been the assumption that producers of
consumers' goods sell their products directly to consumers.
All business units are held, for this reason, to have broadly
parallel interests. Each buys labor and materials, combines
them and passes them along to the public at prices that, in
some sense, maximize returns. Were this in fact the case, the
lot of the consumer would be an unhappy one.

In practice, goods pass to retailers whose interests, normally,[3] are at sharp variance with those of their suppliers. The typical retailer is deeply concerned with his volume of sales. This is uniquely important for minimizing inventory risk, it is a prime factor in the prestige of the concern, and, of course, it is one of the dimensions of profit. The convention that excludes cutthroat price competition — in the case of retailers the cutting of gross margins — is observed by retailers as by other firms. Nonetheless, lower prices — a low level in general as well as low prices in relation to those of other firms — are regarded by one whole class of retailers as the major device for obtaining and maintaining volume. It is in their interest accordingly to resist any exercise of market power by their suppliers that results in higher prices. More important, any power retailers can exercise to reduce their supplier's prices will redound to their benefit. It will enable them to use price as an inducement without breaking the convention against destructive cutting of their own margins.

Such an opportunity exists only when their suppliers are enjoying something that can be taken away, i.e., when they are enjoying the fruits of market power from which they can be separated. Thus, in precise parallel with the labor market, we find the retailer with both a protective and profit incentive to develop countervailing power whenever his supplier is in possession of market power. The practical manifestation of this, over the last half-century, has been the spectacular rise of the food chains, the variety chains, the mail-order houses (now graduated into chain stores), the department-store chains, and the co-operative buying organizations of the surviving independent department and food stores.

This development has been the countervailing response to previously established positions of power. The gains from invading these positions have been considerable. The rubber

[3] An exception of great importance will be stressed presently.

tire industry is a fairly commonplace example of oligopoly. Four large firms are dominant in the market. In the thirties, Sears, Roebuck & Co. was able, by exploiting its role as a large and indispensable customer, to procure tires from Goodyear Tire & Rubber Company at a price from twenty-nine to forty per cent lower than the going market. These it resold to thrifty motorists for from a fifth to a quarter less than the same tires carrying the regular Goodyear brand.

One consequence of the failure of the government to recognize the role of countervailing power is that many hundreds of pages of court records have detailed the exercise of this power by the Great Atlantic & Pacific Tea Company. There is little doubt that this firm has used the countervailing power it has developed with considerable artistry. In 1937, a survey by the company indicated that, for an investment of $175,000, it could supply itself with corn flakes. Assuming that it charged itself the price it then was paying to one of the three companies manufacturing this delicacy, it could earn a modest sixty-eight per cent on the outlay. Armed with this information, and the threat to go into the business which its power could readily make effective, it had no difficulty in bringing down the price by approximately ten per cent.[4] Such gains from the exercise of countervailing power, it will be clear, could only occur where there is an exercise of original market power with which to contend. The A & P could have reaped no comparable gains in buying staple products from the farmer. Committed as he is to the competition of the competitive model, the farmer has no gains to surrender. Provided, as he is, with the opportunity of selling all he produces at the impersonally determined market price,

[4] I am indebted to my friend Professor M. A. Adelman for these details which are from his forthcoming book, on the A & P Case, to be published by the Harvard University Press.

he has not the slightest incentive to make a special price to A & P beyond that which might be associated with the simple economies of bulk sale.

The examples of the exercise of countervailing power by Sears, Roebuck and A & P just cited show how this power is deployed in its most dramatic form. The day-to-day exercise of the buyer's power is a good deal less spectacular but also a good deal more significant. At the end of virtually every channel by which consumers' goods reach the public there is, in practice, a layer of powerful buyers. In the food market there are the great food chains; in clothing there are the department stores, the chain department stores and the department store buying organizations; in appliances there are Sears, Roebuck, and Montgomery Ward and the department stores; these latter firms are also important outlets for furniture and other house furnishings; the drug and cosmetic manufacturer has to seek part of his market through the large drug chains and the department stores; a vast miscellany of consumers' goods pass to the public through Woolworth's, Kresge's and the other variety chains.

In all of these cases buyers deal directly with the manufacturer and there are few of the latter who, in setting prices, do not have to reckon with the attitude and reaction of their powerful customers. The retail buyers have a variety of weapons at their disposal to use against the market power of their suppliers. Their ultimate sanction is to develop their own source of supply as the food chains, Sears, Roebuck, and Montgomery Ward have extensively done. They can also concentrate their entire patronage on a single supplier and, in return for a lower price, give him security in his volume and relieve him of selling and advertising costs.

The more commonplace but more important exercise of countervailing power consists, merely, in keeping the seller in a state of uncertainty as to the intentions of a buyer who is indispensable to him. The larger of the retail buying organizations place orders around which the production schedules and occasionally the investment of even the largest manufacturers become organized. A shift in this custom imposes prompt and heavy loss. The threat or even the fear of this sanction is enough to cause the supplier to surrender some or all of the rewards of his market power. He must, frequently, make a more conditional surrender to less potent buyers if he is not to be more than ever in the power of his large customers. It will be clear that in this operation there are rare opportunities for playing one supplier off against another.

A measure of the importance which large retailing organizations attach to the deployment of their countervailing power is the prestige they accord to their buyers. These men (and women) are the key employees of the modern large retail organization; they are highly paid and they are among the most intelligent and resourceful people to be found anywhere in business. In the everyday course of business, they are considerably better known, both for their capacities and their power, than the salesmen from whom they buy.

There are producers of consumers' goods who have secured themselves from exercise of countervailing power. Some, like the automobile and the oil industry, have done so either by integrating their distribution through to the consumer or because they have an organization of small and dependent and therefore fairly powerless dealers. It seems probable that in a few industries, tobacco manufacture for example, the members are strong enough and have sufficient solidarity to withstand any pressure applied to them even by the most powerful buyer. However, even the tobacco manufacturers, under conditions that were especially favorable to the exercise of countervailing power in the thirties, were forced to make liberal price concessions, in the form of advertising allowances, to the A & P [5] and possibly also to other large customers. When the comprehensive representation of large retailers in the various fields of consumers' goods distribution is considered, it is reasonable to conclude — the reader is warned that this is an important generalization — that most positions of market power in the production of consumers' goods are covered by positions of countervailing power.

Countervailing power also manifests itself, although less visibly, in producers' goods markets. For many years the power of the automobile companies, as purchasers of steel, has sharply curbed the power of the steel mills as sellers. Detroit is the only city where the recently oulawed basing-point system was not used to price steel. Under the basing-point system, all producers regardless of location quoted the same price at any particular point of delivery. This minimized the opportunity of a strong buyer to play one seller off against the other. The large firms in the automobile industry had developed the countervailing power which enabled them to do precisely this. They were not disposed to tolerate any limitations on their exercise of such power. In explaining the quotation of "arbitrary prices" on Detroit steel, a leading student of the basing-point system has recently recognized, implicitly, the role of countervailing power by observing that "it is difficult to apply high cartel prices to particularly large and strong customers such as the automobile manufacturers in Detroit." [6]

The more normal operation of countervailing power in

[5] Richard B. Tennant, *The American Cigarette Industry* (New Haven: Yale University Press, 1950), p. 312.

[6] Fritz Machlup, *The Basing Point System* (Philadelphia: Blakiston Co., 1949), p. 115.

producers' goods markets turns on the relatively small number of customers which firms in these industries typically have. Where the cigarette or soap manufacturer numbers his retail outlets by the hundreds of thousands and his final consumers by the millions, the machinery or equipment manufacturer counts his customers by the hundreds or thousands and, very often, his important ones by the dozen. The latter are important to the seller as individuals and are able to collect the rewards of that importance. As elsewhere, the market pays a premium to those who develop power as buyers that is equivalent to the market power of those from whom they buy. The reverse is true where weak sellers do business with strong buyers.

V

There is an old saying, or should be, that it is a wise economist who recognizes the scope of his own generalizations. While countervailing power is of decisive importance in regulating the exercise of private economic power, it is not universally effective. Some industries, because they are integrated through to the consumer or because their product passes through a dependent dealer organization, have not been faced with countervailing power. As noted, there are a few cases where a very strong market position has proven impregnable even against the attacks of strong buyers. And there are cases where the dangers from countervailing power have, apparently, been recognized and where it has been successfully resisted.

An example of successful resistance to countervailing power is the residential-building industry. No segment of American capitalism evokes less pride. Yet anyone approaching the industry with the preconceptions of competition in mind is unlikely to see, very accurately, the reasons for its shortcomings. There are many thousands of individual firms in the business of building houses. Nearly all are small — the capital of the typical housebuilder runs from a few hundred to a few thousand dollars. The members of the industry oppose little market power to the would-be house owner. Except in times of extremely high building activity there is aggressive competition for business.

The industry does show many detailed manifestations of guild restraint. Builders are frequently in alliance with each other, the unions, and local politicians to protect prices, wages and to maintain established building techniques. These derelictions have been seized upon avidly by the critics of the industry. Since they represent its major departure from the competitive model, they have been assumed to be the cause of the poor performance of the housing industry.

Unhappily, were the restraints on contract prices, materials and techniques in the industry swept away, it seems improbable that the prices of new houses would be much changed and the satisfaction of customers with what they get for what they pay much enhanced. The reason is that the typical builder would still be a small and powerless figure contending with unions that are far stronger than he and buying his building materials in small quantities at high cost from suppliers with effective market power. It is these factors which, very largely, determine the cost of the house.

The builder is kept without power. With few exceptions, the manufacturers of building supplies decline to sell direct to the builder. This prevents any one of the latter from bringing pressure to bear on his source of supply; at the same time it helps keep all builders relatively small and powerless by uniformly denying them the economies of direct purchase. All must pay jobbers' and retailers' margins. A few builders — a spectacular case is Levitt & Sons of Long Island — have managed to circumvent this ban.[7] As the result of more effective buying, a much stronger position in dealing with labor, and the savings from large-scale production of houses, they have notably increased the satisfaction of customers with what they receive for their money. Few can doubt that the future of the industry, if its future is to improve on its past, lies with such firms.

Thus it is the notion of countervailing power, not of competition, which points the way to progress in the housing industry. What is needed is fewer firms of far greater scale with resulting capacity to bring power to bear upon unions and suppliers. It is the absence of such firms, and of the resulting economies, which helps explain why one sector of this industry — low-cost housing where cost is especially important in relation to ability-to-pay — has passed under government management. In the absence of an effective regulating mechanism within the industry in the form of countervailing power, private entrepreneurship has been superseded.

VI

The development of countervailing power requires a certain minimum opportunity and capacity for organization, corporate or otherwise. If the large retail buying organizations had not developed the countervailing power which they have used, by proxy, on behalf of the individual consumer, consumers would have been faced with the need to organize the equivalent of the retailer's power. This would be a formi-

[7] Levitt has established a wholly-owned building-supply company to buy materials for its projects. *Fortune*, August 1947, p. 168.

dable task but it has been accomplished in Scandinavia and, in lesser measure, in England where the consumer's co-operative, instead of the chain store, is the dominant instrument of countervailing power in consumers' goods markets.[8] Quite probably there would have been similar organization in the United States. The fact that there are no consumer co-operatives of any importance in the United States is to be explained, not by any inherent incapacity of the American for such organization, but because the chain stores pre-empted the gains of countervailing power first. The counterpart of the Swedish Kooperative Forbundet or the British Co-operative Wholesale Societies has not appeared in the United States simply because it could not compete with the A & P and the other large food chains. The meaning of this, which incidentally has been lost on devotees of the theology of co-operation, is that the chain stores are approximately as efficient in the exercise of countervailing power as a co-operative would be. (In parts of the American economy where proprietary mass buyers have not made their appearance, notably in the purchase of farm supplies, individuals (who are also individualists) have shown as much capacity to organize as the Scandinavians and the British and have similarly obtained the protection and rewards of countervailing power. The Grange League Federation, the Eastern States Farmers' Exchange and the Illinois Farm Supply Company, co-operatives with annual sales running to multi-million-dollar figures, are among the illustrations of the point.)

However, it must not be assumed that it is easy for great numbers of individuals to coalesce and organize countervailing power. In less developed communities, Puerto Rico for

[8] Especially in Scandinavia the co-operative has been explicitly viewed as a device for countering the power of the cartels — i.e., as an instrument for the exercise of countervailing power.

example, one finds people fully exposed to the exactions of strategically situated importers, merchants and wholesalers and without the apparent capacity to develop countervailing power in their own behalf. (Anyone, incidentally, who doubts the force of the countervailing power exercised by large retailer-buying organizations would do well to consider the revolution which the entry of the large chain stores would work in an economy like that of Puerto Rico and also how such an intrusion would be resented and perhaps resisted by importers and merchants now able to exercise their market power with impunity against the thousands of small, independent and inefficient retailers who are their present outlets.)

In light of the difficulty in organizing countervailing power, it is not surprising that the assistance of government has repeatedly been sought in this task. Without the phenomenon itself being fully recognized, the provision of state assistance to the development of countervailing power has become a major function of government — perhaps *the* major domestic function of government. Much of the domestic legislation of the last twenty years, that of the New Deal episode in particular, only becomes fully comprehensible when it is viewed in this light. To this I shall return in the next chapter.

VII

I come now to the major limitation on the operation of countervailing power — a matter of much importance in our time. Countervailing power is not exercised uniformly under all conditions of demand. It does not function at all as a restraint on market power when there is inflation or inflationary pressure on markets.

Because the competitive model, in association with Say's Law, was assumed to find its equilibrium at or near full employment levels, economists for a long time were little inclined to inquire whether markets in general, or competition in particular, might behave differently at different levels of economic activity, i.e., whether they might behave differently in prosperity and depression. In any case the conventional division of labor in economics has assigned to one group of scholars the task of examining markets and competitive behavior, to another a consideration of the causes of fluctuations in the economy. The two fields of exploration are even today separated by watertight bulkheads, or, more accurately, by professorial division of labor and course requirements. Those who have taught and written on market behavior have assumed a condition of general stability in the economy in which sellers were eager for buyers. To the extent, as in recent years, that they have had to do their teaching or thinking in a time of inflation — in a time when, as the result of strong demand, eager buyers were besieging reluctant sellers — they have dismissed the circumstance as abnormal. They have drawn their classroom and textbook illustrations from the last period of deflation, severe or mild.

So long as competition was assumed to be the basic regulatory force in the economy these simplifications, although they led to some error, were not too serious. There is a broad continuity in competitive behavior from conditions of weak to conditions of strong demand. At any given moment there is a going price in competitive markets that reflects the current equilibrium of supply-and-demand relationships. Even though demand is strong and prices are high and rising, the seller who prices above the going or equilibrium level is punished by the loss of his customers. The buyer still has an incentive to look for the lowest price he can find. Thus market behavior is not fundamentally different from what it is when demand is low and prices are falling.

There are, by contrast, differences of considerable importance in market behavior between conditions of insufficient and excessive demand when there is oligopoly, i.e., when the market has only a small number of sellers. The convention against price competition, when small numbers of sellers share a market, is obviously not very difficult to maintain if all can sell all they produce and none is subject to the temptation to cut prices. Such a device for maintaining the convention against price competition as the basing-point system only has significance when demand is insufficient in relation to capacity. The basing-point system by making known, or easily calculable, the approved prices at every possible point of delivery in the country provided protection against accidental or surreptitious price-cutting. Such protection is not necessary when there is no temptation to cut prices. By an interesting paradox when the basing-point system was attacked by the government in the late depression years it was of great consequence to the steel, cement and other industries that employed it. When, after the deliberate processes of the law, the system was finally abolished by the courts in April 1948, the consequences for the industries in question were rather slight. The steel and cement companies were then straining to meet demand that was in excess of their capacity. They were under no temptation to cut prices and thus had no *current* reason to regret the passing of the basing-point system.

These differences in market behavior under conditions of strong and of weak demand are important and there are grounds for criticizing their neglect — or rather the assumption that there is normally a shortage of buyers — in the conventional market analysis. However, the effect of changes in demand on market behavior becomes of really profound importance only when the role of countervailing power is recognized. Countervailing power, as a restraint on market power, *only* operates when there is a relative scarcity of demand. Only then is the buyer important to the seller and this is an obvious prerequisite for his bringing his power to bear on the market power of the seller. If buyers are plentiful, that is, if supply is small in relation to current demand, the seller is under no compulsion to surrender to the bargaining power of any customer. The countervailing power of the buyer, however great, disappears with an excess of demand. With it goes the regulatory or restraining role of countervailing power in general. Indeed, the best hope of the buyer, under conditions of excess demand, may be to form a coalition with the seller to bring about an agreed division of returns.[9]

Following the useful practice of testing theory against experience, it is worth noting that it was the twenties and the thirties which were the periods of great growth of chain and group buying enterprises.[10] In sharp contrast with most other types of business, the early depression years especially were favorable to the great chain stores. These were years when demand, generally, fell short of the capacity of suppliers to meet it. Thus they were favorable to the exercise of counter-

[9] The everyday distinction between a "buyers" and a "sellers" market and the frequency of its use reflect the importance which participants in actual markets attach to the ebb and flow of countervailing power. That this distinction has no standing in formal economics follows from the fact that countervailing power has not been recognized by economists. As frequently happens, practical men have devised a terminology to denote a phenomenon of great significance to themselves but which, since it has not been assimilated to economic theory, has never appeared in the textbooks. The concept of the "break-even point," generally employed by businessmen but largely ignored in economic theory, is another case in point.

[10] See Temporary National Economic Committee. *Large Scale Organization in the Food Industries*, Monograph No. 35 by A. C. Hoffman (Washington: U.S. Government Printing Office), pp. 5 ff.

vailing power. The intensity of the trade agitation against the mass retailers, culminating in 1936 in the passage of the Robinson-Patman Act (designed as we shall see presently to limit their exercise of this power), was itself a measure of the chain's advantage in this period. By contrast, during the years of strong demand and short supply during World War II, the chain stores lost ground, relatively, to independents. As this strong demand in relation to supply destroyed their capacity to exercise countervailing power, their advantage disappeared. It is interesting to note that the trade agitation and resentment against the chains almost completely disappeared during the war and postwar years.

However, it is again in the labor market where the change in the pattern of exercise of countervailing power that accompanies changes in demand can be seen with greatest clarity. Here also it has the most portentous consequences. In industries where strong firms bargain with strong unions, the management of the former has what has come to be considered a normal resistance to wage increases when demand is not pressing upon capacity. To yield is to increase unit costs. The firm cannot with impunity pass along these higher costs to its customers. There may be a question as to whether other firms in the industry will follow suit; there will always be a question of the effect of the higher prices on sales. If the demand for the products is in any measure elastic the consequence of the higher prices will be a loss of volume. This, with its effect on employment in the industry, is something of which modern union leadership, as well as management, is usually conscious. Thus the trial of strength between union and management associated with collective bargaining is, essentially, over the division of profits. When demand is limited, we have, in other words, an essentially healthy manifestation of countervailing power. The union opposes its power as a

seller of labor to that of management as a buyer: At stake is
the division of the returns. (An occasional strike is an indication that countervailing power is being employed in a sound
context where the costs of any wage increase cannot readily
be passed along to someone else. It should be an occasion for
mild rejoicing in the conservative press.) The *Daily Worker*,
eagerly contemplating the downfall of capitalism, should
regret this manifestation of the continued health of the
system.

(Under conditions of strong demand, however, collective
bargaining takes on a radically different form. Then management is no longer constrained to resist union demands on the
grounds that higher prices will be reflected in shrinking
volume.) There is now an adequate supply of eager buyers.
The firm that first surrenders to the union need not worry
lest it be either the first or the only one to increase prices.
There are buyers for all. No one has occasion, as the result
of price increases, to worry about a general shrinkage in
volume. A strong demand means an inelastic demand. On
the other hand, there are grave disadvantages for management
in resisting the union. Since profits are not at stake, any time
lost as the result of a strike is a dead loss. Worker morale
and the actual loss of part of the working force to employers
who offer better wages must be reckoned with. Thus when
demand is sufficiently strong to press upon the capacity of
industry generally to supply it, there is no real conflict of
interest between union and employer. It is to their mutual
advantage to effect a coalition and to pass the costs of their
agreement along in higher prices. Other buyers along the
line, who under other circumstances might have exercised
their countervailing power against the price increases, are
similarly inhibited. Thus under inflationary pressure of
demand, the whole structure of countervailing power in the
economy dissolves.

We have already seen an example of this dissolution of countervailing power in the continuing rounds of wage and price increases following World War II. The full coalition between management and labor, under the conditions of inflationary demand of these years, was partly disguised by the conventional expressions of animosity and by the uncertainty of management as to how long the inflation would last. However, the "Fifth Round" in 1950–51 was negotiated with scarcely an important strike. The President of the United States Steel Corporation, in yielding to the union in November 1950, indicated a *de facto* coalition when he pointed out that the "half-cent" inflation in steel prices, which would be passed along to customers, was a small price to pay for "uninterrupted and expanded" production. The consequences of this failure of countervailing power in times of inflation are considerable and I shall return to a fuller consideration of them in the final chapter. First, however, it is necessary to examine the role of the state in the development of countervailing power.

CHAPTER X

Countervailing Power and the State

IN THEIR RELATIONS with government, the American people
have long shown a considerable ability to temper doctrine by
pragmatism. The ruggedly conservative businessman who
excoriates Statism, the Welfare State and the State Department, does not allow his convictions to interfere with an application to the RFC if he really needs the money. The im-
peccably conservative business journal which editorially con-
demns Keynesians and deficit spending as heralds of disaster
does not fail to point out on the financial page that the effect
of the new budget, which it so deplores, will be favorable to
business volume and earnings. The up-country cotton or
tobacco planter whose belief in States' rights is unequaled
except by his mistrust of civil rights votes, nonetheless, for
federally administered marketing quotas, a remarkably comprehensive form of agricultural regimentation.

Since the phenomenon of countervailing power is of great
practical importance, even though it has gone unrecognized
in economic or political theory, we should expect, in line
with our highly pragmatic approach to government, that it
would have been the object of a good deal of legislation and
the subject of a good deal of government policy. As the last
chapter has made clear, there are strong incentives in the
modern economy for developing countervailing power.

Moreover, the group that seeks countervailing power is, initially, a numerous and disadvantaged group which seeks organization because it faces, in its market, a much smaller and much more advantaged group. This situation is well calculated to excite public sympathy and, because there are numerous votes involved, to recruit political support.

In fact, the support of countervailing power has become in the last two decades perhaps the major peacetime function of the federal government. Labor has sought and received it in the protection and assistance which the Wagner Act provided to union organization. Farmers sought and received it in the form of federal price supports to their markets — a direct subsidy of market power. Unorganized workers have sought and received it in the form of minimum wage legislation. The bituminous-coal mines sought and received it in the Bituminous Coal Conservation Act of 1935 and the National Bituminous Coal Act of 1937.[1] In a considerably more tenuous sense, investors have received it, via the Securities and Exchange Commission, in support of their position vis-à-vis the management or control of the large corporation. These measures, all designed to give a group a market power it did not have before, were among the most important legislative acts of the New Deal.

There should be no problem as to why this legislation, and the administration that sponsored it, were keenly controversial. The groups that sought the assistance of government in building countervailing power sought that power in order to use it against market authority to which they had previously been subordinate. Those whose power was thereby inhibited could hardly be expected to welcome this development or the intervention of the government to abet it.

---

[1] The first Act was declared unconstitutional in 1936; the second was allowed to expire during the war.

Because the nature of countervailing power has not been firmly grasped, the government's role in relation to it has not only been imperfectly understood but also imperfectly played. One is permitted to hope that a better understanding of countervailing power will contribute to better administration in the future.

II

The role of countervailing power in the economy marks out two broad problems in policy for the government. In all but conditions of inflationary demand, countervailing power performs a valuable — indeed an indispensable — regulatory function in the modern economy. Accordingly it is incumbent upon government to give it freedom to develop and to determine how it may best do so. The government also faces the question of where and how it will affirmatively support the development of countervailing power. It will be convenient to look first at the negative role of the government in allowing the development of countervailing power and then to consider its affirmative role in promoting it.

At the outset a somewhat general distinction — one that is implicit in the discussion of the last chapter — must be made between countervailing and original power.[2] When, anywhere in the course of producing, processing or distributing a particular product, one or a few firms first succeed in establishing a strong market position they may be considered to be the

[2] William J. Fellner in his interesting recent book, *Competition among the Few: Oligopoly and Similar Market Structures* (New York: Alfred A. Knopf Co., 1949), observes that the market power of unions, in relation to that of corporations, is of a neutralizing not an additive character. It will be evident, I think, that this involves a distinction similar to the one I am making.

possessors of original market power. They are able, as the result of their power over the prices they pay or charge, to obtain more than normal margins and profits.[3] These are at the expense of the weaker suppliers or customers. This is the monopoly position anciently feared by liberals and as anciently condemned by economists. Their instincts were sound. Countervailing power invades such positions of strength, whether they be held by suppliers or customers, and obtains a share in the rewards.

The rule to be followed by government is, in principle, a clear one. There can be very good reason for attacking positions of original market power in the economy if these are not effectively offset by countervailing power. There is at least a theoretical justification for opposing all positions of market power. There is no justification for attacking positions of countervailing power which leaves positions of original market power untouched. On the contrary, damage both in equity and to the operation of the economy will be the normal consequence of doing so.

The problems of practical application of such a rule are mostly in the field of the antitrust laws and they are a good deal more difficult than the simple articulation of the rule implies. However a general distinction between original and countervailing power is, in fact, now made in the antitrust laws — it has been forced, against the accepted current of ideas concerning competition, by the practical reality of the phenomenon itself.

In the first development of positions of market power, a long lead was assumed by industrial corporations. Thus, when workers and farmers sought to develop strength in the sale of their labor power and products, they did so in markets where industrial firms had already achieved positions of orig-

[3] Technically prices or margins in excess of marginal costs.

inal power. It would be broadly in harmony with the distinction between original and countervailing power to exclude labor and farm organizations from prosecution under the antitrust laws. This has been done. While the Sherman Act made no mention of labor, Congress did not have in mind the still modest efforts of unions to lift their bargaining power when it enacted the legislation in 1890. Subsequently, unions became subject to the law by judicial interpretation. Indeed, in the first few decades that the legislation was in effect, unions were a primary target. This led to their exclusion by name in the Clayton Act of 1914. After the Supreme Court had somewhat obdurately reincluded them in 1921 (Justices Brandeis, Holmes and Clarke dissenting) they were again and finally excluded by the Norris-LaGuardia Act of 1932 and by the subsequent and more benign decisions of a New Deal Court.

Similarly, efforts by farm co-operatives to enhance the market power of the farmer, so long as they are held within reason, are excluded by the Clayton Act of 1914, by further legislation (the Capper-Volsted Act) in 1922 and in more specific instances by the Agricultural Marketing Agreement Act of 1937. Congress has thus recognized, implicitly, that the efforts of labor and agriculture to develop market power were different from those of industrial firms. The difference — the only plausible difference — was that these efforts were the response of workers and farmers to the power of those to whom they sold their labor or products.

A more precise and conscious use of the distinction between original and countervailing power would take account of the fact that some trade unions and some farm groups are clearly the possessors of original power. Thus workers in the building trades, although they are not highly organized or exceptionally powerful in any absolute sense, are strong in relation to the small-scale employers with whom they do business. They are clearly the possessors of original market power. The special nature of their power, as compared with that of the trade-union movement generally, explains the distress of men and women who have reacted sympathetically to the role of unions in general but who, in this case, have found themselves on the side of organizations that have plenary power to restrict output and enhance their own income. The obvious solution lies in the distinction between original and countervailing power. This, logically, would make restrictive practices of master plumbers or plasterers a proper object of interest by the Department of Justice while the absolutely (though not relatively) far more powerful unions in steel or automobiles who impose no similar restrictions on the supply of their labor would not be.[4]

Similarly, there are undoubted cases of exercise of original power by groups of agricultural producers. The immunity granted by existing law is not complete — the Secretary of Agriculture is authorized to enter a complaint if, as result of the activities of the co-operative, prices are "unduly enhanced," and a co-operative cannot merge its power with non-agricultural corporations. As a result there have been a scattering of prosecutions of farmer's organizations — of the California Fruit Growers' Exchange (Sunkist Oranges) and of a Chicago milkshed producers' organization in combination with distributors, unions and even a college professor. But such cases have been infrequent.

However, the more serious consequences of the failure to

---

[4]Again, government policy has shown a tendency to recognize, pragmatically, distinctions which are not recognized in the available theory. In 1940 the original power of the building trades unions was attacked by the Department of Justice. However, by eventual decision of the Supreme Court — *U.S.* v. *Hutcheson et al*, 312 U.S. 219 (1940) — the unions were held to be substantially immune.

perceive the role of countervailing power have been within the fabric of industry itself. The antitrust laws have been indiscriminately invoked against firms that have succeeded in building countervailing power, while holders of original market power, against whom the countervailing power was developed, have gone unchallenged. Such action has placed the authority of law on the side of positions of monopoly power and against the interests of the public at large. The effects have been damaging to the economy and also to the prestige of the antitrust laws.

As the last chapter has made clear, one of the most important instruments for exercise of countervailing power is the large retail organization. These are the public's main line of defense against the market power of those who produce or process consumers' goods. They are an American counterpart — and without doubt an effective one — of the consumer co-operatives which, in other countries, are viewed as an instrument for countering the power of the cartels. Yet the position of the large retail organizations has been not only a general, but also in some measure a unique object of government attack. Chain stores and other large buyers have been frequent recent objects of Sherman Act prosecution and are the special target of the Robinson-Patman Act which is especially designed to inhibit their exercise of countervailing power.

Under the provisions of the Robinson-Patman Act a chain store may receive the benefit of the demonstrably lower costs of filling the large orders which it places; it may not receive concessions that are the result of its superior bargaining power. The effect, since these concessions are important only when won from positions of original economic power, is to discriminate in favor of original power and against countervailing power.

The effects of failure to distinguish between original and countervailing power have been especially noteworthy in the several suits against the Great Atlantic and Pacific Tea Company. This company was prosecuted before the war for violation of the Robinson-Patman Act,[5] was convicted of violation of the Sherman Act in a case brought in 1944 and finally decided in 1949 [6] and is defendant in a further action now before the courts. In spite of its many legal misadventures, the company has not been charged with, or even seriously suspected of, exploiting the consumer. On the contrary, its crime has been too vigorous bargaining, which bargaining was, effectively, on the consumer's behalf. In the case brought in 1944 it was charged with seeking to increase its volume by reducing its margins and with bringing its bargaining power too vigorously to bear upon its suppliers in order to get price reductions. These suppliers — which included such powerful sellers as the large canning companies — had long been involved in a trial of strength with A & P over prices. They were left undisturbed. The government was in the highly equivocal position of prosecuting activities which have the effect of keeping down prices to the consumer. The positions of market power, which had given A & P its opportunity, were left untouched.

The litigation against A & P has been strongly defended. Although the firm does rather less than ten per cent of the food-retailing business, has strong rivals, and is in an industry where the entry of new firms is singularly easy, much stress has been laid on the danger that it might achieve an effective monopoly of food-retailing. Nevertheless one can hardly

[5] *Great Atlantic & Pacific Tea Co.* v. *FTC*, 106 F. 2d 667 (1939).
[6] *U.S.* v. *New York Great Atlantic & Pacific Tea Co.*, 67 F. Supplement 626 (1946). For a discussion of this case see M. A. Adelman, "The A & P Case: A Study in Applied Economic Theory," *Quarterly Journal of Economics* (May 1949), pp. 238 ff.

doubt that these cases have been a source of serious embarrassment to friends of the antitrust laws. No explanation, however elaborate, can quite conceal the fact that the effect of antitrust enforcement, in this case, is to the disadvantage of the public. Viewed in light of the present analysis the reason becomes evident. The prosecution by inhibiting the exercise of countervailing power provides protection to the very positions of market power that are anathema to the defender of the antitrust laws.[7]

No one should conclude, from the foregoing, that an exemption of countervailing power should now be written into the antitrust laws. A considerable gap has always separated useful economic concepts from applicable legal ones. However, a number of conclusions, with immediate bearing on the antitrust laws, do follow from this analysis. In the first place the mere possession and exercise of market power is not a useful criterion for antitrust action. The further and very practical question must be asked: Against whom and for what purposes is the power being exercised? Unless this question is asked and the answer makes clear that the public is the victim, the antitrust laws, by attacking countervailing power, can as well enhance as reduce monopoly power.

Secondly, it is clear that serious damage can be done to the

---

[7] Much of the pressure for the Robinson-Patman Act and its enforcement (and in lesser measure also the state Fair Trade laws which have a similar ultimate effect) came and continues to come from the smaller competitors of the chains who do not themselves have effective countervailing power. They have, in effect, sought to protect their own weaker buying position by denying strength to others. This is wholly understandable but it has not been the only recourse of the independent. He has had the alternative of joining his bargaining power, as a buyer, with other independents. And, in some fields — food-retailing and department stores for example — such co-operative bargaining has enjoyed a large measure of success. A clearer view of original and countervailing power by public authority would also have made this the preferred way of protecting the position of the independent retailer.

economy by such legislation as the Robinson-Patman Act. This legislation is the culmination of a long and confused legal and legislative struggle dating from 1914 over what economists have come to call price discrimination. The ostensible motive of the legislation is to protect competition. The seller is prevented from giving a lower price to one customer than to another where the lower price cannot be justified by the economies associated with the particular sale and where the effect is "to injure, destroy, or prevent" competition either with the seller or between his customers. The practical effect, reinforced by recent court decisions, is to make any important price concessions to any large buyer of questionable legality.[8]

Even those who are unwavering in their belief in competition have been inclined to doubt whether this legislation does much to protect competition. What is not doubtful at all is that the legislation strikes directly at the effective exercise of countervailing power. To achieve price discrimination — to use bargaining power to get a differentially lower price — is the very essence of the exercise of countervailing power. In trying, with questionable effect, to preserve one of the autonomous regulators of the economy the government is seriously impairing another.

Finally, the theory of countervailing power throws important light on the advantage of different numbers of firms in an industry and on the objectives of the antitrust laws in relation thereto. One of the effects of the new ideas on market theory, as noted in Chapter IV, was to raise serious doubts whether an industry of small numbers was, in fact, socially preferable to a monopoly. Once firms had recognized their

----

[8] Especially *FTC* v. *Morton Salt Company*, 334 U.S. 37 (1948) although a still more recent decision makes legitimate concessions to meet the price of another seller (*Standard Oil of Indiana* v. *FTC* 71 S. Ct. 240, 1951).

interdependence, it was believed that they would find a price, output and profit position not greatly different from that which would be achieved by a single firm. This made it doubtful whether it was worth while to prosecute a monopoly in order to create an oligopoly.

The high technical dynamic of the typical industry that is shared by a few firms will already have raised some questions about this conclusion. There is reason to suppose that such an industry will be more progressive than an industry controlled by one. Recognition of the role of countervailing power suggests a further clear advantage on the side of the oligopoly. One can hardly doubt that, in general, it will be much easier for countervailing power to break into a position of market strength maintained by an imperfect coalition of three, four or a dozen firms than into a position held by one firm. When there is more than one firm in a market there are opportunities for playing one off against another. Such opportunities abruptly disappear when the number is reduced to one.

Thus the theory of countervailing power comes to the defense of the antitrust laws at what has been a very vulnerable point. Efforts to prevent or to disperse single-firm control of an industry can be defended for the greater opening they provide for the exercise of countervailing power. Similar and equally good reasons exist for resisting mergers. Those who have always believed there was something uniquely evil about monopoly are at least partly redeemed by the theory of countervailing power.

III

It must surely be agreed that, during the present century, American economic and political life have gained in strength as the result of the improved position of workers and farmers — two previously disadvantaged groups. In contrast with the sullenness and anger of labor relations or the deep-seated sense of frustration and inferiority of Midwestern farmers of a scant fifty years ago, both groups now have a well-developed sense of confidence and equality. These attitudes have a solid foundation in material well-being. It would seem difficult for anyone to argue that the American economy or polity is anything but stronger as a result.

The government has played an important part in this development. Both farmers and workers have sought and received government assistance, either in the form of direct support to their market power or in support to organization which in turn made market power possible. In short the government has subsidized, with its own power, the countervailing power of workers and farmers. (The efforts on behalf of agriculture reveal so many facets of the problem of countervailing power that they are worth examining in some detail. This is done in the next chapter.) This assistance, clearly, explains some part of the self-confidence and well-being which these groups display today.

Yet few courses of policy have ever been undertaken more grudgingly and with a greater sense of guilt. One can scarcely imagine a government action which, on the record, has produced more beneficent results in practice in which less pride has been taken. Especially in the case of agriculture, all measures have, until recently, been characterized as "emergency" legislation. This is invariably our label for excusing to our consciences action which seems to be at once wise and unwise.

The reason for this sense of guilt is that the notion of a government subsidy of its power to groups seeking to develop countervailing power has never enjoyed a place in the accredited structure of American economic and political science. Accordingly the unfinished tasks of developing such power have never had a place on the reformer's calendar. The reformer, in fact, has almost invariably been overtaken by the action. When the groups in question have developed enough influence to obtain government assistance on their own behalf they have simply gone ahead and got it without blessing or benefit of doctrine.

What has strengthened the American economy so admirably in the past must be presumed to have an unexploited potential for good in the future. There are still some millions of Americans who are without any organized expression of market power and whose standards of living and welfare are categorical evidence of the consequences. These include, for example, the 2.3 million hired farm workers, the truly forgotten men of American life. They have no security in their employment — there are few that cannot be fired on a day's notice. They do not have unemployment insurance; they are normally unprotected by workmen's compensation in what is a fairly hazardous occupation; many do not have a fixed place of abode; their pay, even in times when there is a strong demand for their services, is far from handsome. A share in the gains from the newly developed market power of the farmer has still to be transmitted to his hired man.

There are also the unorganized urban workers, those on the fringes of the labor movement and, perhaps most important of all, occupational categories which, in the past, have foresworn efforts to develop economic power. Schoolteachers, clerical workers, municipal employees and civil servants have generally avoided organization as something not quite genteel or because it was believed that employers and the community at large would recognize their importance and pay accordingly. In addition the natural leaders among white-collar workers have had, as ordinary workers do not, the clear alternative of obtaining promotion. A ten per cent increase in pay is not of great consequence to a high-school mathematics teacher if he is soon to become principal. This self-denying ordinance by white-collar workers where organization is concerned has invariably been viewed with approval, even as a manifestation of patriotism and sound Americanism, by public authorities and private employers.

Quite possibly the white-collar groups did not suffer too severely from their lack of market power in the years before World War II. In times of stable prices the salaried worker seeks an increase in pay only for the sake of increasing his real income. His weakness is not likely — as with the wage earner contending against pay cuts — to cost him ground. A skillful negotiator can do much for himself.[9] However, in times of rising prices such as we now face and perhaps face for the future, market power will have to be exercised affirmatively if past positions are to be held. It seems to me quite probable — and since the end of the war there have already been indications of a trend — that the next group to seek to assert its market power will be the genteel white-collar class. In any case, we cannot assume that efforts by presently unorganized groups to seek market power, and to seek the assistance of government in their effort, is finished business.

In the actual sequence of events, some measure of organization by the group themselves must precede any very important government subsidy to their developing market

---

[9] Though clearly this is not a simple business. The psychological crisis of the devoted but unassertive white-collar employee when he must appeal for a salary raise is one of the most reliable topics of the American cartoonist. The popularity of the theme, apart from revealing the intransigeant sadism of cartoonists and their audience, suggests that the problem depicted is a real one.

power. Not until farmers and workers achieved some organization on their own behalf were they able to get the state to
reinforce their efforts. In the thirties the Farm Security
Administration, an idealistic and imaginative effort to help
subsistence and tenant farmers and farm workers, largely
petered out because those aided lacked the organization to
defend in Congress and before the public the efforts being
made on their behalf. Support to countervailing power is not
endowed, *ad hoc*, by government. It must be sought.

IV

At this point it becomes possible to answer, at least tentatively, one of the questions with which this essay was
launched. That is the meaning of the great expansion of
state activity in recent decades — the expansion which conservatives have found so alarming and which many liberals
have supported without knowing quite why. We can now
see that a large part of the state's new activity — the AAA,
the Wagner Act, minimum-wage legislation — is associated
with the development of countervailing power. As such it
is neither adventitious nor abnormal; the government action
supports or supplements a normal economic process. Steps
to strengthen countervailing power are not, in principle, different from steps to strengthen competition. Given the existence of private market power in the economy, the growth
of countervailing power strengthens the capacity of the economy for autonomous self-regulation and thereby lessens the
amount of over-all government control or planning that is
required or sought.

Two or three further points may be made. Increasingly, in
our time, we may expect domestic political differences to

turn on the question of supporting or not supporting efforts
to develop countervailing power. Liberalism will be identified
with the buttressing of weak bargaining positions in the economy; conservatism — and this is its proper function — will
be identified with the protection of positions of original
power. There will be debate over whether weak positions
have been unduly strengthened. The struggle over the Taft-
Hartley Act is an example of the kind of political issue which
countervailing power can be expected to develop. The essential question at issue in the Taft-Hartley controversy was
whether, in the process of buttressing a weak bargaining
position, the government had turned it into an unduly strong
one. One is inclined to suppose that popular indignation
with the current claims of some farm groups reflects the
feeling that a bargaining position that was once unduly weak
has now been made unduly strong.

On the whole, the appearance of countervailing power as
a political issue cannot be considered especially unhealthy
although it will almost certainly be so regarded. At first
glance there is something odious about the notion that the
poor and the excluded improve their lot in a democracy only
by winning power. There is something even more odious
about the suggestion that the state can usefully have a part
in the process. But so far, at least, there has been less reason
to regret than to approve the results of such a policy. The
life of farmers and workers, the two great groups that have
enjoyed the most obvious subsidy of power, has evidently
been improved. It is hard to say that the community at large
has suffered.

The concern over economic power is always less a matter
of the way it is manifested than of how it *might* be employed.
This is an area where anything that is novel has an unparalleled aspect of danger. A leading American industrialist

warned in 1903 that: "Organized labor knows but one law and that is the law of physical force — the law of the Huns and the Vandals, the law of the savage. . . . Composed as it is of the men of muscle rather than the men of intelligence, and commanded by leaders who are at heart disciples of revolution, it is not strange that organized labor stands for principles that are in direct conflict with the natural laws of economics." [10] Not even the professional alarmist would voice such views of the labor movement today. It is only in light of history that our fear of the countervailing power of weaker groups dissolves, that their effort to establish their power in the market emerges as the stuff of which economic progress consists. It is by our experience, not our fears, that we should be guided.

[10] David M. Parry, President of the National Association of Manufacturers. Annual Address. New York *Times*, April 15, 1903.

CHAPTER XI

The Case of Agriculture

THE EFFORT of longest standing to develop countervailing power, not even excepting that of labor, has been made by the farmer. And his efforts have taken a striking diversity of forms. Because of its importance in itself, and because of the light it throws on the problem of building countervailing power, the case of agriculture is worth examining in more detail.

In both the markets in which he sells and those in which he buys, the individual farmer's market power in the typical case is intrinsically nil. In each case he is one among hundreds of thousands. As an individual he can withdraw from the market entirely, and there will be no effect on price — his action will, indeed, have no consequence for anyone but himself and his dependents.

Those from whom the farmer buys and those to whom he sells do, characteristically, have market power. The handful of manufacturers of farm machinery, of accessible fertilizer manufacturers or mixers, of petroleum suppliers, of insurance companies all exercise measurable control over the prices at which they sell. The farmer's market for his products — the meat-packing industry, the tobacco companies, the canneries, the fluid-milk distributors — is typically, although not universally, divided between a relatively small number of large companies. There is no more vigorously debated question in economics than that of the measure of jurisdiction that such companies exercise over their buying prices. That a measure of latent power exists for tacit or overt influence over such prices can hardly be denied. A canning factory must, after all, declare the price it will pay on a given day or during a given week or season for tomatoes. Implicit in such power of decision is some measure of influence over the price and the influence will be increased if the factory is the only one in the area or if it has a shrewd judgment as to the probable behavior of other buyers. But even where the influence is difficult to see, it may be inherent in the greater ability of the buyer to decide to buy or not to buy. This, in turn, can have considerable effect on prices. The farmer has no equivalent discretion.

In our time, partly as a result of the new market power of the farmer and partly as a reaction to his very considerable political influence, the market power of those to whom he sells has come to be exercised with profound circumspection. This has not been true in the past. On the contrary, the farmer was often made to pay dearly for his lack of market power. It was this that led him to search long and hard for a formula for expressing effective countervailing power.

II

Indeed, the effort is nearly as old as settlement on this continent. Within a few years after the first colonists arrived in Virginia, the tobacco planters were petitioning the Crown for redress against the oppression of the "unconscionable and cruel merchants" who bought their tobacco and supplied

them with goods from England.[1] In 1631 the colonial authorities stipulated that no tobacco might be offered for purchase
of English goods at a valuation of less than sixpence a pound.
The tobacco growers, for the first but not the last time, were
seeking the support of public authority in an effort to bolster
their bargaining position against their more powerful customers and suppliers. The result was the first but not the
last support price for farm products in North America. The
circumstances which motivated it were not different from
those that led to the New Deal farm program almost exactly
three centuries later. In both cases the tobacco producers
were seeking to redress the organic inequalities of bargaining
power in a market where the many face the few.

It might be added that this first support price had other
consequences which later experience has made familiar. The
colonial authorities were speedily forced on from price to
production control. In 1639, a primitive Agricultural Adjustment Act established a maximum production for that and
the two following years of 1,200,000 pounds. Viewers were
appointed to secure compliance on the individual plantations
and given plenary authority to burn inferior grades of tobacco and up to one-half of any planter's crop.[2] Regimentation of the farmer, Secretary of Agriculture Brannan will be
charmed to learn, did not originate with the Brannan Plan.

As the analysis of the last two chapters suggests, there are,
in principle, three things which the farmer can do to offset
his weakness in bargaining power. He can seek to build
countervailing power in the market — in the tradition of the
Virginia tobacco planters. Or he can seek to dissolve the
original power of those to whom he sells or from whom he

---

[1] L. C. Gray, *Agriculture in the Southern United States to 1860* (Washington: Carnegie Institution, 1933), vol. I, p. 430.
[2] *Ibid.*, p. 261.

buys. Finally, he can attempt to get the advantages of the enhanced market power that are associated with changes in demand. To the extent that demand in the economy as a whole can be maintained at strong or inflationary levels, his position as a seller will be strong. This results from the shift of power from buyer to seller under conditions of inflation which, in relation to its effect on countervailing power, was examined in Chapter IX. Like other producers, the farmer is more disposed to emphasize his role as a seller than as a buyer and there are very good reasons why he should do so.

American farmers have tried all three methods of buttressing their market power. Under agrarian pressure the northern colonies, especially before the middle of the eighteenth century, were inveterately inflationist. The colonies of the Middle Atlantic were considerably less given to inflation but only, apparently, because stronger governors prevented the issue of paper money. The southern colonies, with some exceptions such as South Carolina, had comparatively stable currencies.[3] In these latter colonies, which depended heavily on their export trade in staples, there was no appreciable advantage to the farmers in inflation. The English sterling prices of tobacco and goods were what counted; these were beyond the reach of colonial monetary policy.

During much of the nineteenth century — successfully when Jackson was his candidate,[4] unsuccessfully when it was

---

[3] Cf. Richard A. Lester, *Monetary Experiments* (Princeton: Princeton University Press, 1939), p. 24.

[4] My colleague, Professor Arthur M. Schlesinger, Jr., has warned me against implying that Jackson himself was an inflationist. His supporters were; so were the effects of his successful attack on the Second Bank of the United States. However, Jackson himself was a conservative in monetary matters and indeed the exponent of a hard-money policy. His opposition to the Bank and to Nicholas Biddle arose not from the restraint they exercised on the inflationary note issues of the state banks but from the conviction that they had too much power.

William Jennings Bryan — the farmer concentrated his efforts on expanding demand. Through the free banking of the Jacksonian era and the free coinage of Bryan, as well as in such shorter-lived episodes as the Greenback Movement in the seventies, he sought to increase the means of payment and therewith to alter the balance of bargaining power in his favor. Historians have all but invariably related this inflationary bias of the nineteenth-century agrarian to his desire to ease the burden of his indebtedness. This explanation, in its neglect of the issue of relative bargaining power, is almost certainly incomplete.

In this century the farmer has largely lost interest in inflation. One reason is that inflation has ceased to be technically practicable by the old methods. With modern banking institutions and modern attitudes of borrowers and lenders, borrowing does not follow automatically when credit is available as it very nearly did in the time of Jackson. The volume of bank borrowing and the resulting movements in money supply have now become consequences, not causes, of other changes. As a result, the possibility of deliberately engineering an old-fashioned credit or currency inflation has disappeared. Inflation can still be brought about through the agency of large budget deficits, but these do not have the aura of easy costlessness of unlimited emissions of banknotes or unlimited coinage of silver. The frustrations of the Bryan campaigns, and the growing suspicion of the green magic of the money doctors, gradually weaned farmers away from their old faith in monetary experiment. As this happened, they turned to more forthright methods of equalizing their bargaining power.

Initially, this took the form of efforts to break down the market position of those with whom the farmer did business. In the latter part of the nineteenth century and in the early decades of the present century, by far the strongest pressure for the regulation or dissolution of big business came from the farmbelt. The first and most spectacular manifestation of this was the Granger Movement. With almost revolutionary venom, the farmers of the early seventies turned on the railroads, commission merchants, warehousemen, farm machinery companies and merchants with whom they did business. In seeking regulation of these enterprises the Grangers saw, quite clearly, that they possessed market power which the farmer did not have. To quote the historian of the movement, "Just as the price which the farmer received for the commodities he sold seemed to him to be fixed by those to whom he sold, so also, he felt that the price of his supplies was fixed by those from whom he bought." [5]

The Granger eruption was short-lived. It flared across Illinois, Iowa, Wisconsin and the Eastern Great Plains, capturing state legislatures and passing laws to bring railroads, warehouses and other enterprises under state control. But it soon succumbed to individualism and inexperience and to corrupt leadership. It was, however, the precursor of a considerably more durable effort to dissolve opposing market power. Farmers, far more than labor, the urban middle class or any other group including the liberal intellectuals of the day, forced the passage of the Sherman Anti-Trust Act of 1890. It is perhaps not entirely an accident that meat packers, tobacco companies, the farm-machinery industry, milk distributors and, in earlier days, the railroads, all of whom buy from, sell to or serve the farmer, have been prominent targets of this legislation. During its sixty-year history, the strongest regional support for the Sherman Act and its supplementing legislation has come from the farm states. How-

[5] Solon J. Buck, *The Granger Movement* (Cambridge: Harvard University Press, 1913), p. 18.

ever, this legislation can no longer be considered central in the farmer's strategy for equalizing market power. The Sherman Act and subsequent antitrust legislation still enjoy the support of farm organizations and, generally, of Western congressmen. But it reflects a passive and even somewhat nostalgic interest. Farmers have turned from the reduction of opposing market power to the building of their own.

III

In seeking to develop countervailing power it was natural that farmers would at some stage seek to imitate the market organization and strategy of those with whom they did business. For purchase or sale as individuals, they would seek to substitute purchase and sale as a group. Livestock or milk producers would combine in the sale of their livestock or milk. The market power of large meat packers and milk distributors would be matched by the market power of a large selling organization of livestock producers and dairymen. Similarly, if purchases of fertilizer, feed and oil were pooled, the prices of these products, hitherto named by the seller to the individual farmer, would become subject to negotiation.

The necessary instrument of organization was also available to the farmer in the form of the co-operative. The membership of the co-operative could include any number of farmers and it could be democratically controlled. All in all, the co-operative seemed an ideal device for exercising countervailing power. For a period in the twenties and early thirties there was a widespread belief among American farmers that marketing co-operatives were indeed the answer to their needs. Following the depression of 1921, a remarkable propa-

gandist from California, Aaron Sapiro, pictured for the co-
operative member precisely the kind of bargaining position
enjoyed by the processor or manufacturer. " . . . We have
stopped dumping in the State of California and have substituted the merchandising of agricultural products. That
means centralized control of these crops so that they move
to such markets of the world, and at such times, as the
markets can absorb the crops at fair prices." [6] Sapiro-type
co-operatives, as they came to be called, were formed to
market potatoes, tobacco, wheat, fruit and other products.
Few survived, as bargaining instruments, for more than a
year or two.

As a device for getting economies of larger-scale operations
in the handling of farm products or for providing and capi-
talizing such facilities as elevators, grain terminals, warehouses and creameries, co-operatives have enjoyed a considerable measure of success. For exercising market power
they have fatal structural weaknesses. The co-operative is a
loose association of individuals. It rarely includes all producers of a product. It cannot control the production of its
members and, in practice, it has less than absolute control
over their decision to sell. All these powers over its own
production are possessed, as a matter of course, by the corporation. A strong bargaining position requires ability to
wait — to hold some or all of the product. The co-operative
cannot make the non-members wait; they are at liberty to
sell when they please and, unlike the members, they have
the advantage of selling all they please. In practice, the co-
operative cannot fully control even its own members. They
are under the constant temptation to break away and sell
their full production. This they do, in effect, at the expense

[6] Ontario Department of Agriculture, *Addresses on Co-operative Marketing by Mr. Aaron Sapiro* (Toronto, 1922).

of those who stand by the co-operative. These weaknesses destroyed the Sapiro co-operatives.

The farmer's purchasing co-operative is free from the organic weaknesses of the marketing or bargaining co-operative. In the marketing co-operative the non-co-operator, or recusant, gets a premium for his non-conformance. In the buying co-operative he can be denied the patronage dividends which reflect the economies of effective buying and bargaining. In the purchase of feed, chemicals for fertilizers, petroleum products and other farm supplies and insurance these co-operatives have enjoyed major success. As earlier noted, they have come to rank with the mass retailers as instruments for the effective expression of countervailing power. However, they redress the weakness of his position only as a buyer and only for part of his purchases. Their success in nowise compensated for the failure of the marketing co-operative as a bargaining instrument.

The failure of the voluntary co-operative as a device for expressing market power is important, for out of it, by remarkably direct steps, grew the agricultural programs of the thirties. After the farmer had failed to organize market power by himself, it was wholly in the tradition of the development of countervailing power that he should turn to the government for assistance. And it was equally natural that the government should first think of helping the farmer to establish the kind of co-operatives which, by his unaided efforts, he had been unable to build. This was done in the Agricultural Marketing Act of 1929. The Federal Farm Board established under this legislation undertook to sponsor and capitalize a system of national co-operatives. The bargaining powers of the latter were, in turn, to be supplemented by government Stabilization Corporations.

Had this effort been successful, wheat, cotton, tobacco and

other farm producers would have been represented in their markets by one or a few powerful sellers. Their power in such markets would not have been different in kind from that already enjoyed by the steel companies, the automobile companies or the Aluminum Company of America in theirs. It is appropriate that this legislation was enacted by a Republican Administration in which American business attitudes were dominant. Faced with the need for doing something for the farmer, the obvious course to Mr. Hoover and his colleagues was to remake the farmer as nearly as possible in the image of the typical industrial corporation.

The co-operatives hastily synthesized by the Federal Farm Board were subject to the same weaknesses — they placed the same premium on non-conformance and had the same inability to control the output of either member or non-member — as the voluntary co-operatives. Both they and the Stabilization Corporations were also engulfed by the price collapse of 1930 and 1931. In 1933 the victorious Democrats put the power resources of the government fully at the disposal of agriculture. In one sense this was but a small additional step. The Agricultural Adjustment Act of 1933, and the subsequent agricultural legislation, merely eliminated the technical weakness which had led to the failure of the earlier voluntary or government-aided efforts. The now half-forgotten processing tax of the original legislation was levied against the production of all growers of basic crops.[7] The proceeds were distributed to those who submitted to control of production. By penalizing the non-co-operator and so controlling production of all, the weaknesses of voluntary bar-

[7] So called. Initially wheat, cotton, corn, hogs, rice, tobacco and milk and milk products were so designated although all were not subject to the tax. See Edwin G. Nourse, Joseph S. Davis, and John D. Black, *Three Years of the Agricultural Adjustment Administration* (Washington: The Brookings Institution, 1937), p. 42.

gaining through the co-operative were eliminated. After the abandonment of the processing tax in 1936 (when it was declared unconstitutional), direct subsidies from the Treasury, paid only to co-operators, were used as a passive penalty on the non-participant. In more recent times government purchases or loans have provided price guarantees which, if supplies are large, are contingent on the willingness of producers to accept marketing quotas on what they sell. This again is a change of form, not of content; by offering itself as an alternative customer, the government is still engaged in the essential task of reinforcing the bargaining position of the farmer.

Such, in brief, is the extraordinarily consistent record of the farmer's efforts to develop countervailing power. Curiously enough, the whole effort is still viewed, even to some extent by farmers themselves, as vaguely artificial. While the word "emergency" has now disappeared from agricultural legislation, there is still a subjective feeling that some day it will pass away. The fact that the modern legislation is now of two decades' standing, that behind it is a long history of equivalent aspiration, that there is not a developed country in the world where its counterpart does not exist, that no political party would think of attacking it are all worth pondering by those who regard such legislation as abnormal.

So far from being abnormal, given the market power of the industries among which the American farmer is cited and the probability of fluctuating demand, it is organic. There would be many advantages in recognizing this. If we fail to regard government support to the bargaining power of the farmer and other groups as normal, we shall almost certainly neglect to search for the principles that should govern the subsidy of private groups by public power. We shall also be less likely to correct the considerable number of abuses which have been associated with government aid to countervailing power — abuses which have been especially numerous and serious in agricultural legislation. Many who might have concerned themselves with these faults have continued to suppose that the remedy is to abolish the entire activity. Like the executioners during the French Revolution, they have offered the guillotine as a cure for headache. This is not the best frame of mind in which to seek improvement in what is certain to continue.

CHAPTER XII

The Role of Decentralized Decision

THE TIME has now come to apply the argument of the last
several chapters to what has been the most heated subject of
domestic controversy in the United States in recent decades,
namely the role of the state in relation to private economic
decision. In the past, private business management has had
decisive responsibilities in the economy. It has decided what
to produce, in what quantity, at what price, paying what
wages and with what investment to increase future production. In addition it has had the responsibility for organizing
and managing production. Whether the decisions required
in these tasks be difficult or simple, a great many decisions
are required. The most distinctive characteristic of the businessman — the thing that most sharply distinguishes him
from the lawyer, college professor or, generally speaking, the
civil servant — is his capacity for decision. The effective
businessman is invariably able to make up his mind, often on
limited evidence, without uncertainty as to his own wisdom.
It is a part of this talent not to reflect on past mistakes or
even to concede that a mistake has been made.

The presumption of a rule of competition in the economy
led to the further presumption that these business decisions
would be at least generally in the public interest. Poor decisions or mistakes harmed the businessman, not the public;

good decisions benefited all. As a result, state interference
with business decision was either redundant or positively
harmful. With the increasing implausibility of the assumption of competition, the ancient basis for the businessman's
claim to independence became subject to serious erosion.
The question that now arises is to what extent independent
business decision is rehabilitated when countervailing power,
not competition, is recognized as a restraint on the private
exercise of economic power? When this is answered there
still remains the further question as to what interference with
the businessman's autonomy is required, not to prevent the
misuse of power, but to insure that the economy finds its peacetime norm without too much unemployment or too much
inflation? This chapter takes up the role of the state in relation to private market power; the two final chapters of this
essay examine its role in relation to general economic performance and stability.

II

The phenomenon of countervailing power does provide a
strong negative justification for leaving authority over production decisions in private hands. Like competition countervailing power operates to prevent the misuse of such power.
The firm or group of firms that is using its market power to
enhance prices or depress wages, as the last three chapters
have shown, both force and reward the development of the
strength that neutralizes such power. If this did not happen,
private decisions could and presumably would lead to the
unhampered exploitation of the public or of workers, farmers
and others who are intrinsically weak as individuals. Such
decisions would be a proper object of state interference and

would soon so become. This interference is now made unnecessary because those affected by the decisions are able, in effect, to look after themselves.

Since the development of countervailing power is irregular and incomplete, it does not provide a blanket case for the exclusion of state interference with private decision. Moreover the state must be expected to participate in the development of countervailing power. Nonetheless, it is countervailing power which, in the typical modern market, regulates the power of private decision. As such it provides the negative justification for leaving decision in private hands, for it prevents these decisions from working harm on others.

I venture to suggest that this rationale of private authority over production — or of private enterprise — will be almost equally unpalatable to liberals and conservatives. This is often the case with reality. Liberals will almost certainly detect here a nefarious whitewash of crypto-monopoly and bigness. They are reminded, however, that they also have here the explanation of why, in a triumph of conscience and pragmatism over doctrine, they themselves have so often turned up, so inconsistently, on the side of trade unions, farm legislation and other efforts to build seeming monopoly power.

To conservatives this argument should be attractive. In resting their case for private authority over production decisions on competition, they have had all the tactical mobility of a rider whose horse has been shot out from under him. The statistics of market concentration are notably unfavorable to their case. There is the opposing weight of modern market theory. This receives verification from the observably tenuous, nonexistent or distorted character of competition in many markets — plus the highly visible preference of businessmen, as Walter Lippmann once noted, for as little of it as possible. Socialists have not been slow to detect and exploit the tactical weaknesses of the conservative case. In the Marxian lexicon, capitalism and competition are mutually exclusive concepts; the Marxian attack has not been on capitalism but on monopoly capitalism. The fact that that power of the genus of monopoly is ubiquitous has not been difficult to show. So long as competition remains the conservative's defense, the left is bound to have a near monopoly of the evidence and the logic.

However, I cannot think that conservatives will find a defense of private decision that rests on countervailing power wholly pleasant. It makes indispensable the market power of unions, farmers, mass buyers and others. Like competition this power is uncomfortable whenever it is effective. The present analysis also legitimatizes government support to countervailing power. This is certain to be regarded for some time to come as an undesirable extension of state activity even though it is already a commonplace one. I hazard the guess that the leader of the average large corporation will, for a time, prefer the implausible defense that he is a competitor in the classical sense, a mere barometer of market pressures, to the plausible one that his power, though considerable, is deployed against others who are strong enough to resist any harmful exercise of such power. There is nothing an economist should fear so much as applause, and I believe I am reasonably secure.

III

The foregoing deals only with the negative case for private authority over production decisions. It is negative, for it shows only the resistance to a damaging exercise of private market power where there is a full development of countervailing power. In the competitive model there was a strong affirmative case for private production decision. Competition produced the most efficient use of resources; any interference by the state with private decisions concerning production could not therefore be beneficial and must accordingly be harmful.[1] In the early part of this century classical and socialist economists wrangled at length over the question of whether a planned economy could devise any method of distributing resources and for accounting for costs of production that would be an effective substitute for what occurred under the price system. Even socialists were inclined to concede that the case for socialism stood or fell on their ability to do so.

No case for an *ideal* distribution and employment of resources — for maximized social efficiency — can be made when countervailing power rather than competition is accepted as the basic regulator of the economy. Countervailing power does operate in the right direction. When a powerful retail buyer forces down the prices of an industry which had previously been enjoying monopoly returns, the result is larger sales of the product, a larger and broadly speaking a more desirable use of labor, materials and plant in production. But no one can suppose that this happens with precision. Thus a theoretical case exists for government intervention in private decision. It becomes strong where it can be shown that countervailing power is not fully operative.

In our time there has been a considerable and very possibly a growing tendency to criticize private business decision. This has been manifested in recent months — as I write — in dissatisfaction with decisions of the steel industry on prices

---

[1] There were always some theoretical exceptions, among them instances of long-run decreasing costs and of wide divergencies between private and social costs of production.

and on provision of new capacity, with the general performance of the housing industry, even with the price and design
of automobiles. There is no a priori reason to suppose that
this criticism is ill founded. It cannot be argued that the undisturbed judgment of the industry in these cases is necessarily the best one; the social judgment, reflected in the attitudes of government, may well be theoretically better.

It has been shown, however, that technical development
may compensate, or more than compensate, for more evident
shortcomings of private decision and that wealth provides us
with some latitude in these matters. Much more important,
there is a strong administrative case for private decision.

Although little cited, even by conservatives, administrative
considerations now provide capitalism with by far its strongest defense against detailed interference with private business
decision. To put the matter bluntly, in a parliamentary
democracy with a high standard of living there is no administratively acceptable alternative to the decision-making
mechanism of capitalism. No method of comparable effectiveness is available to decentralize authority over final decisions.

Even where the concentration of control over industry is
relatively great, the final authority over production decisions
is held at a comparatively large number of points. This is
of great significance. The decisions of the General Motors
Corporation on the power, design, price, model changes, production schedules, and the myriad of other details concerning its automobiles are final. There is no appeal; the career
or reputation of no higher authority is at stake. Were there
such recourse, the process of reaching final decisions in a
modern economy with a wide variety of products would be
almost incredibly difficult. To deny the right of resort to
ultimate authority would be to deny, from within the fabric

of government, an accepted democratic right, that of free petition.[2]

The process of decision-making has two dimensions — timing and quality. For relatively simple and undifferentiated types of production — the production of electric power for example — the quality of the decision is normally more important than its timeliness. There the administrative problems of public management can be solved. Quite the reverse is true of consumers' goods. A poor decision is normally to be preferred to a late one. Any considerable centralization of authority over the decisions that are required in the production of the great variety of American consumer products — over what to produce, of what design, when, where and with what investment for each — is something that it would seem hard for even an ardent socialist to contemplate. It can be argued that decentralization of decision might be possible — and might eventually be accepted even by a people and a legislature accustomed to the full rights of appeal — for all except key decisions. Only questions of wages, prices and the broad contours of production and investment would be subject to central design. This is possible and for certain larger objectives of economic stabilization a broadly parallel pattern of action may be necessary. But such a proposal really misses the point. The objective of social control over production decisions is to make the resulting decisions more responsive to social needs and desires. If, for administrative reasons, government, having centralized decision, must then put the decision-making outside the reach of public opinion and pressures, it has abandoned the very job which it set out to perform.

2 Were the state the manufacturer of automobiles, I for one would insist on the right to appeal against their present design which seems admirably suited only to a race of recumbent midgets. Presumably the midgets would want, then, to enter their brief in opposition.

Because the debate over socialism and planning has turned so heavily on such economic considerations as incentives and possibilities of accounting and pricing, these administrative considerations have been largely overlooked. Yet there is every indication that in our time they are decisive. If, as here argued, any substantial degree of central authority over production decisions is administratively impossible in a community with a high, variegated and variform standard of living, then the corollary is that such planning may be entirely feasible in a community with a fairly primitive standard of living. Centralized decision would become administratively possible where production is confined to a relatively small number of relatively standard products. Checking once more with experience, one finds it is communities with a low and simple standard of living — Russia, Eastern Europe and now China — that have turned (or been turned) to socialism. The advanced industrial countries, by contrast, have not done so even where they have an ideological commitment to socialism. There is a popular cliché, deeply beloved by conservatives, that socialism and communism are the cause of a low standard of living. It is much more nearly accurate to say that a low and simple standard of living makes socialism and communism feasible.

The decisive role of administration in countries with high living standards is admirably illustrated by the Scandinavian countries, and by the glacial gradualism with which socialist governments in these lands have proceeded toward public ownership. The recent history of the United Kingdom is even more instructive. The depth of the commitment of the British masses to central planning is not open to question nor is the sincerity of their leaders. In no other country, perhaps not even in Russia, was capitalism more thoroughly defeated as an idea among a voting majority of the people than in

Britain after the thirties. But both the pace and form of British socialism when it came to power were sharply circumscribed by the problems of administering it. After the Labour victory in 1945, it soon became evident that the rate at which industries would be taken into public ownership would be determined primarily by administrative considerations. A growing appreciation of the scale and complexity of the administrative apparatus required not only slowed the pace of nationalization but also, it would appear, tempered the enthusiasm of British socialists for the policy itself.

The effect of administrative considerations on the selection of industries to be nationalized has been even more interesting. The first block of industries marked for nationalization — coal-mining, transport, electricity, gas utilities, overseas communications and the Bank of England — were, with the exception of the first, ones in which public ownership involved a minimum of administrative difficulty or even of change. Public ownership of these industries is commonplace in advanced industrial countries. These industries were familiar socialist targets; it would be unfair to suggest that they were consciously selected because they would be easy to manage. But the fact that they presented no insurmountable administrative problems was almost certainly a passive factor in their selection. More can be said of the industries now tentatively on the Labour Party's docket for nationalization. While there is some special history of legislation or agitation in the case of both, sugar-refining and cement manufacture must surely have looked attractive because of the comparative ease with which they could be managed.

On the other hand, the Labour Government left the consumer industries — automobiles, radios, clothing, textiles and the like — severely alone. Here any centralization of authority over production decisions — decisions that would reflect, in their number, the variety of products and the need for accommodating production, design and style to the shifting tastes of consumers at home and abroad — would be most difficult. It can be assumed that few British leaders, whatever their political convictions, wished to shoulder such responsibilities. Thus, though no British Labour Member and not all Conservatives profess any affection for capitalism, it survives because of the absence of any administratively feasible alternative.

It is the same considerations, coupled with the restraints of countervailing power, that protect the American businessman in his present authority. In excluding full state control over his decisions, they do not, of course, preclude all interference with private decision. This remains a strictly pragmatic matter, to be settled on its merits in the individual case. In industries, electric-power utilities for example, where market power is inherent in the structure of the industry and where the development of countervailing power cannot be expected by the great mass of consumers,[3] government control of private decision must be expected. The fact that decision-making in such industries has been shown to be well within the competence of public authority makes possible the further step toward public ownership — a step that has become commonplace in the United States. In other industries — low-cost housing for example — government management can be readily justified even though the decisions involved are numerous and difficult. Here effective countervailing power has not developed and the product in question is of peculiar importance. The administrative problems created by centralization do not put the advocate of government intervention or

[3] It is noteworthy that large users, by the development of standby plant, by the threat to move or by other assertions of their indispensability as a buyer are frequently able to develop effective countervailing power even in this field.

of public ownership out of business. They do, in combination with the theory of countervailing power, direct and in a measure confine his energies to those industries and areas where there is a genuine need for his remedy. He must, and this is a reasonable demand, bear the burden of proving that the centralization of decision which his program requires justifies the administrative problem which it creates.

IV

Clearly, even the great administrative problems of public ownership might have to be tackled and surmounted were the alternative continuing malperformance like that of the thirties or the persistent inflation that was experienced following World War II and with which we may again have to contend. The resolution of the problem of market power does not resolve these questions. We have, within the economy, no mechanism which acts autonomously to insure proper performance; it is sadly evident from experience as well as from theory that the peacetime norm of the American economy is not necessarily stability at a high level of production and employment. This latter, clearly, is taken as a desideratum by a great majority of Americans. The last task of this book is to see what assertion of state power, and what interference with private authority, is necessary to have high and reasonably stable production, employment and prices.

CHAPTER XIII

The Role of Centralized Decision

THE AMERICAN TRADITION in economics involves a remarkable balance of candor and conservatism. It is sufficiently candid to keep the American businessman constantly alarmed about the ideas of economists but sufficiently conservative to make the alarm unwarranted. In this tradition, American economists have expressed deep and continuing alarm over the problem of private market power. But they have rarely looked with favor on comprehensive government interference with private business decisions.

On the contrary, they have engaged in an avid search for a formula for correcting the shortcomings in the behavior of the economy while leaving private authority over production decisions unimpaired. There has been, in modern times, something close to an agreed formula for achieving this aim. Economists have hoped, many against hope, that competition, backed as necessary by rigorous enforcement of the antitrust laws, would serve to maximize social efficiency and prevent the abuse of private power in the market. Meanwhile inflation and depression, the larger failures in performance, would be taken care of by the further formula identified with the name of Keynes.

The eagerness with which Keynes' doctrines were discussed by American economists, following the publication of

his last great book in 1936,[1] is to be explained as much by the
urgency of the dilemma from which he provided a seeming
escape as by the plausibility of the solution itself. For there
was a very great difference between the urgency of the questions of social efficiency and market power associated with
the abandonment of the competitive model and those presented by the depression. The first were important princi-
pally in the realm of ideas. Competition seemed not to be
effective but the consequences, for reasons that have now been
adequately explored in this book, seemed not to be disastrous.
But the depression really existed; to find a remedy for it was
a categorical imperative.

The essence of the Keynesian formula consists in leaving
private decisions over production, including those involving
prices and wages, to the men who now make them. The businessman's apparent area of discretion is in nowise narrowed.
Centralized decision is brought to bear only on the climate in
which those decisions are made; it insures only that the
factors influencing free and intelligent decision will lead to
action that contributes to economic stability. Thus, in times
of depression, increased government expenditures or decreased taxation will cause or allow an increase in demand.
The resulting business decisions on production and investment, though quite uncontrolled, will result in increased production and employment.

In time of full or overfull employment and rising prices the
course of uncontrolled decisions, which otherwise would be
in the direction of increasing prices and wages, will be re-
shaped by higher taxes and lower government expenditures.
These latter will make sales difficult. Price increases will be
unwise; so will decisions to expand investment and employ-

[1] *The General Theory of Employment, Interest and Money* (New York:
Harcourt, Brace and Co., 1936.)

ment. In this way the government, by influencing the total demand for goods, gets the pattern of decision which it seeks without at any stage intervening in the decision itself.

There are many questions of method raised by such a policy and for fifteen years economists have debated them vigorously. What are the relative advantages of increasing government expenditures or reducing taxes for getting an increase in demand? To what extent can the increase in expenditure or the reduction in taxes be made automatic? (Unemployment compensation payments, for example, are automatic for they increase automatically with a decline in employment.) Is it possible to anticipate inflation or deflation or must action be taken after the fact? How much unemployment or inflation can be tolerated? All this accepts the policy and concerns itself only with application. The chief doubt about the policy itself which the generality of economists have permitted themselves in recent years is whether the government can have, not the intelligence, but the will to carry through the policy. To increase taxes and cut government expenditures to halt inflation has been supposed, in particular, to be peculiarly challenging to a politician.

If the Keynesian formula is workable, then the last of the major reasons for alarm over American capitalism dissolves. The economy, in peacetime, can be kept somewhere close to an equilibrium of capacity production or (the more common synonym) to full employment. There will still be some reluctance to concede this large responsibility to government. For some, Keynes will doubtless remain a sinister figure, more dangerous even than the classical symbols of dangerous thoughts, Darwin, Bryan and Marx. But not everyone can be happy. And even among businessmen there is, as noted earlier, a wide acceptance of Keynes. The Committee for Economic Development, the newest and in respect of ideas the most influential of national business organizations, has a deep though unproclaimed commitment to Keynes.[2] More-over, were acceptance of Keynes unanimous it would be un-fortunate for his followers. For fifteen years they have been able to wear a mantle of radicalism that has been unique in all history in its comfort. Their prophet, a self-made mil-lionaire, sought for nothing so earnestly as to save liberal capitalism. His followers were equally persuaded of their mission. They could thus claim that they were being at-tacked for their efforts to preserve the *status quo*; they were martyrs to their own enlightened conservatism.

II

Given peace, and also freedom from the *force majeure* of large expenditures for armed forces, considerable confidence could be placed in the Keynesian formula. We could expect it to work because we could look forward to the kind of economy in which it is capable of working. Unhappily the prospect is not so favorable. Although Keynes provided a plausible solution to the problem of deflation and depression, the application of his formula to the economy is not sym-metrical. It does not deal equally well with the problem of inflation.

This has not been fully recognized. Economists, like busi-nessmen, farmers and workers, have, as noted, been subject to

[2] Cf. *Jobs and Markets*. By the C.E.D. Research Staff. (New York: Mc-Graw-Hill Book Co., Inc., 1946.) Although a staff study, this book appears to reflect fairly the trend of C.E.D. thinking on economic stabilization. An N.A.M. study, while disapproving of the use of government expendi-tures for stabilization, does endorse the Keynesian equivalent of variable tax rates. Rates would be increased in good times, reduced during depres-sion. *The American Individual Enterprise System*. Economic Principles Commission. (New York: McGraw-Hill Book Co., Inc., 1946), p. 982.

the depression psychosis. As a result, discussion of what has come to be called Keynesian fiscal policy has been, in practice, mostly a discussion of policies to counter depression. The problem of controlling inflation has been dismissed, far more frequently than has yet been realized, by the assumption that it requires measures that are the equal and opposite of the depression remedies. On close examination, and when the role of countervailing power in the economy is recognized, this turns out to be not the case. And, unfortunately, inflation, not depression, is the greatest present and well may be the most persistent future tendency of the American economy. However, it will be convenient, first, to examine the application of the Keynesian formula to depression.

In the years after 1945 the American people lived in almost month-to-month expectations of a disastrous collapse in prices, production and employment. It is now possible to say, with the always invaluable aid of hindsight, that a serious depression was never possible in these years. This was partly the result of continuing high military expenditure. However unfruitful this was in armed strength, it was large and, in combination with foreign-aid programs, aid to veterans and the vast postwar boom in our great nationalized industries of dam-building and ditch-digging, it provided a secure flow of spending to supplement private demand. The dollar total of federal expenditures alone in 1947 was rather more than a third as great as all expenditures, public and private, in 1929. It was more than a half as great as all expenditures in 1932. None of this government expenditure was subject to the kind of sudden cessation which might characterize private investment and which would bring a contraction or a collapse in demand. It was wholly reliable.

In addition, in these years, there was a vastly greater reliance than hitherto on corporate and personal income taxes. The yield of both these taxes at given rates increases or decreases more than proportionately with an increase or decrease in business activity. The personal income tax, since it reflects the movement of people up to higher or down to lower tax brackets, has an especially strong tendency of this sort. Thus it cuts more deeply into private demand the more excessive the demand, and frees it for private use in larger amounts, the larger the drop in demand. It is doubtful, incidentally, if any single device has done so much to secure the future of capitalism as this tax. It is regarded, in our time, as the great leveler of incomes. But the income tax is also — a much neglected point — the great buttress of inequality. The rich man no longer has the embarrassing task of justifying his higher income on grounds of superior morals, ability, diligence or higher natural right. He need only point to the tax he has to pay. And the man of modest income now reflects that his relative poverty saves him a terrifying tax bill. As an added dividend, the tax works silently and automatically on the side of economic stability. Conservatives should build a statue to it and to its inspired progenitor, President William Howard Taft.

Important steps toward stabilization were also in existence as a consequence of, or as a reaction to, the miseries of the thirties. Unemployment insurance secured the worker a minimum of income while out of work. Knowledge of this enabled him to spend his current income with the assurance that he would have some source of livelihood in event of depression. Had there been a considerable reduction in employment, there would have been a resulting floor (although a low one) under a considerable part of consumer expenditure. Farm support prices assured the commercial farmer of rather more than minimum prices (and income) should prices fall. Government expenditures to support farm prices would have risen automatically and astronomically had there been a considerable decline in demand. As a result farmers' spending would have remained fairly stable. Within a short space of ten years a very large amount of stability had been built into the aggregate of expenditures in the economy.

At the same time it remained fairly evident that the American economy needed such props. In 1947 and 1948, the first full years of freedom from wartime controls, there was an extraordinary pressure of demand. Consumers sought the goods they had been denied during the war — or in the depression years before — and had high current incomes, their wartime savings and a generous supply of consumer credit with which to make their wants effective. Their expenditures increased by over $50 billion — from $123 billion to $179 billion — from 1945 to 1948.[3] To consumer demand, plus demand for new housing, was added the demand of business concerns. After 1945 business firms sought to recoup the depletion and obsolescence of the wartime years (and of the thin years before) and to accommodate their plant to the growth in the economy and the new technology that had come with the war. The annual total of all domestic investment by private firms (including investment in housing) reached $45 billion in 1948; in 1929 it was $15.8 billion and in 1932 a mere $900 million.[4]

These extraordinary demands on the economy produced an inflation of some magnitude: the consumer's price index, on its 1935–39 base of 100, was 139 in 1946, 159 in 1947, 171 in 1948, and at the end of that year leveled off at 169 where, with minor changes, it remained through 1949. These price increases were extremely uncomfortable for those whose in-

[3] Economic Report of the President, Council of Economic Advisers, January, 1950.
[4] *Ibid.* This is gross private investment.

comes did not rise. They had a damaging effect on schools, colleges, welfare institutions and public services, all of peculiarly vital importance to a democracy. They also seriously weakened the faith of the American people in government bonds. Millions had a lesson in what happens to the purchasing power of such fixed income-bearing assets in time of inflation. But, in view of the magnitude of the claims on the economy in these years, it can only be a matter for surprise that the price increases, in the absence of controls or a determined tax policy to minimize their effect, were as small as they were. As Professor Alvin Hansen has said:

> The remarkable thing about the period from the end of the Second World War to the Korean crisis is . . . that, notwithstanding the large backlog of deferred demand for plant, equipment, houses, and consumers' durables, and despite the vast military and foreign aid programs, the American economy, after a catching-up period of only a couple of years, proved fully equal to the task. This was a tremendous demonstration of how vast a volume of aggregate demand is necessary to keep the . . . American economy fully employed.[5]

In 1949 the American economy, with the great bulge of postwar demand apparently digested, settled back into a mild but nonetheless quite unmistakable depression. Unemployment, which was a mere 1.6 million in October, 1948, rose to about 4 million the following July.[6] However, this downward trend reversed itself well prior to the Korean war.

[5] *Business Cycles and the National Income* (New York: W. W. Norton Co., 1951), pp. 507–8.
[6] Economic Report of the President.

III

Taking a full view, the behavior of the economy in these years was decidedly encouraging for those who have come to rely on the Keynesian formula. A sudden and very large increase in consumer and business demand was accommodated at the cost of a substantial though not disastrous inflation. In the absence of this restocking demand and also perhaps of some of the arms and foreign-relief expenditures, one can be reasonably certain that the tendencies in the economy would have been deflationary rather than inflationary. In other words the way in which the great bulge in private demand, together with the considerable volume of public demand, was met suggests that in the absence of these abnormal pressures, the economy would have had to be propped rather than restrained.

As emphasized in Chapter IX,[7] under conditions of deflationary pressure, the internal regulators in the economy work as they are supposed to work. The countervailing power of buyers can be brought to bear on sellers; that of workers is brought to bear on employers without the danger of a coalition between the two parties that passes the costs of the settlement along to the public. The experience of the years from 1945 to 1950 showed that the economy possessed what may loosely be termed a deflationary potential. Its tendency was to behave in such manner that the internal regulators would function and with efficiency.

At the same time the experience of these years showed that the economy could be sufficiently propped up so that there would be no disastrous depression. In short, it was made clear that props would work. The twelve billion dollars spent for the armed forces and the four and a half billion

[7] See pp. 133 to 139.

spent for foreign aid in the twelve months preceding the outbreak of the Korean war, a period of essentially stable prices
and something less than full employment, held the economy
closer to full employment than it would have otherwise remained. Had the world been completely at peace, the same
funds spent for roads, housing, the inevitable ditches and
dams of the Corps of Engineers and the Reclamation Service,
for assistance to underdeveloped countries and by consumers
who had become the beneficiaries of well-designed tax reductions, would have had an equivalent propping effect.

A tendency for the American economy to require propping, rather than repressive measures to control demand, has
— as noted — the overwhelming advantage that, under such
circumstances, the regulative force of countervailing power
remains at work. An additional virtue is that the needed
action is in the main stream of American politics. The necessary tax and expenditure policies have the approval of workers and farmers. As a matter of principle they are approved
by a good many businessmen and as a matter of practice,
where their own markets are involved, by a good many
more. Neither an increase of expenditure nor a reduction in
taxes places the average Congressman in political jeopardy.
The bureaucracy faces both without dismay. Standing
against such action in the past has been, only, a barrier of
ideas — the idea that such action, and the unbalance of revenues and expenditures which resulted, violated the canons
of fiscal sanity. Given Say's Law and a tendency for the
economy to find its equilibrium at full employment, such action to support demand was not only unnecessary but positively harmful. Anyone who questions the power of ideas
should consider how successfully, for how long and against
what political odds, convictions based on Say's Law held the
fort against the notion that budgets might wisely be unbal-

anced during depression. But Say has finally been dethroned.

In this period decentralized business decision, which I have identified as the pivotal feature of American capitalism, remained substantially unimpaired. Speaking with all the caution that broad generalization requires, the experience of these years suggests that there are no problems on the side of depression or deflation with which the American economy and polity cannot, if it must, contend.

CHAPTER XIV

Centralized Decision and Inflation

THIS BOOK, if it ended here, would indeed end on a happy note. The lives of a whole generation of Americans have been dominated by the fear of depression. A reading of recent experience has suggested that the American economy is unlikely soon to find, on the side of depression and deflation, any problems with which it cannot contend and none which would require an extension of the scope of centralized decision beyond the impersonal guidance provided by the Keynesian formula. Moreover the same experience of the years between 1945 and 1950 would lead one to expect that it would be against deflation that, most probably, the Keynesian formula would have to be invoked. There are some hitherto unsuspected virtues in deflation. We know it can be countered; it provides the context in which the internal regulators work best. Thus we have a formula which insures a favorable over-all performance of the economy; that formula involves no revolutionary or even very drastic change in the economy or the relation of government thereto; the outlook is for the moderate deflationary tendencies in which both the economy and the formula can be expected to function well.

In one sense the task of this book — the task which was set in the first chapter — is now finished. That task was to examine into the substance our alarms concerning the Amer-

ican economy in the years following World War II. This
has been done. The not unhappy result is that many of our
worries of these years do, on closer examination, dissolve.
The ruling ideas of the period were better designed to maximize our alarm than our understanding of the economy.

II

However, we are not to be left without troubles. I have
shown only that the Keynesian formula is a plausible counter
to deflation and depression. As this book goes to press (in
the summer of 1951) military expenditures are increasing
rapidly. There has also been a considerable modification of
the depression psychosis. People who once held money or
its equivalent in the fear of depression have been seeking to
hold goods in the fear of inflation or shortages. The combined effect of this public and private demand may well be
a long-continued pressure on the productive capacity of the
economy. Accordingly, inflation must now be considered
not a possibility but a probability.

Inflation poses a far more serious threat to decentralized
decision than does depression. When there is inflation, as
noted, the self-regulatory mechanism based on countervailing power, ceases to be effective. It takes on, instead, a
malignant form which becomes part of the dynamic of inflation itself. As demand for goods increases, and becomes increasingly inelastic, those who are exercising countervailing
power on behalf of buyers are no longer able to make their
power effective. The balance between those who are exercising it on behalf of sellers and their customers is upset. The
consequences, especially in the labor market are profound.
Employers who are faced with demand for higher wages can

pay them and pass the added cost along in prices with impunity. They do. The higher wages become, in turn, the source of the higher income which helps sustain demand at the new prices. What, under all conditions of deflationary pressure, is an admirable device for countering the power of buyers of labor becomes a device for accelerating and perpetuating inflation.

This interaction of wages upon prices and prices upon wages has, it must be emphasized, a dynamic of its own whenever production is at or near the current capacity of plant and the labor force. A comparison of the market regulated by countervailing power with the market of the competitive model will show the nature of this self-agitating movement. A net increase in total demand, in an economy regulated by competition, will, in the short run, bring a proportionate increase in prices. Prices will rise to the point where, when multiplied by the currently available production, the value of the available supply will equal total demand. There will be no further effects within the period in which total output cannot be appreciably increased. A further increase in prices will require a further net increase in demand. The whole process is smoothly reversible. A reduction in net demand equal to the preceding increase will bring a like reduction in prices. All this holds equally whether the starting point be, by some historical standard, from a position of high demand or low. Wages of workers will rise and fall smoothly, and purely as a consequence of the movements in prices.

Where markets are regulated by countervailing power, by contrast, a net increase in demand at any time when the labor force and plant are being used to approximate capacity brings a further train of consequences. As noted, both labor and management are in a position to seek and obtain increases in prices or wages. It makes little difference which takes the initiative, one forces the other to follow. An initial wage increase for labor means higher costs for management. These provide a need, or a justification, for price advances. An initial price advance by management means higher profits and, prospectively at least, higher living costs for labor. These provide both an incentive and a justification for wage demands.

In the nature of man, if for no other reason, both labor and management will normally seek something more than mere compensation for the last change to their disadvantage. Thus, as has been well demonstrated by recent experience, management after paying a wage increase will recoup something more than the resulting cost increase in prices. The result is an increase in profits which, along with the further increase in living costs, remains as a kind of residual incentive to labor to start the next round.

There is no definite limitation on the magnitude of the price and wage increases in any of these rounds. This depends, quite indeterminately, on the accident of the bargain that is struck — more accurately the coalition that is reached — between management and labor.

With the competitive model, as noted, the increase in price associated with a given net addition in demand is proportional. With countervailing power and the economy working at the capacity of plant and labor force, the increase in prices may, depending on the accident of the bargain, be less, just, or more than proportional. With the competitive model the increase in price follows the increase in demand and that is the end of it. With countervailing power the initial impulse sets in motion a further train of impulses going further in the same direction. With the competitive model, the process was smoothly reversible; a decrease in demand brought a proportionate decrease in prices. With countervailing power, demand may decrease but, if there is still pressure on capacity, prices will continue to rise. Prices will not be certain to fall until the reduction in demand is sufficient to cause production to be less — perhaps rather substantially less — than current capacity. When the economy is regulated by countervailing power, the relation of current levels of production to the current capacity of plant and labor force is of fundamental importance.

As a practical matter, both under the competitive model and with countervailing power, a continuing upward movement of prices requires continuing additions to demand beyond that made available by current production. A government deficit, consumer expenditures from past savings, a continuing increase in business and consumer bank borrowing or some combination of all these is necessary to sustain the movement. However, where there is countervailing power the net addition need only be sufficient to hold production at or near capacity. This may not need to be very great. Much of the requisite addition to demand can, indeed, be supplied as a concomitant of the wage and price increases.[1]

The force of this interaction of wages on prices and prices on wages is partly, but only partly, lessened by the fact that important components of the cost of living — most notably food, and in practice also houseroom and much clothing — are not immediately affected by increased wages. These are set in competitive markets where there is no immediate response by prices to an increase in costs. Thus the effect of wages, via costs on prices and back on wages by way of the

[1] This is evident in the case of wage income and is especially important because the increased wage income in some measure anticipates the price increases which result in its absorption. Elsewhere in the economy, especially in the management of inventories, the price increase induces or even forces increases in income, the source of which is either corporate dissaving or increased bank loans.

cost of living, is not quite as direct as appears at first glance. Nevertheless, we must reckon on a continuing interaction of wages on prices whenever demand is pressing on the capacity of the economy.

III

In addition to the prospective pressure of demand from defense expenditures, there is now a further danger of greatly increased demand as the result of a decision by the American people that inflation is part of their future. Largely as a result of World War II, and the methods of war finance then employed, the public at large is in possession of a large volume of liquid or spendable assets. The total of their holdings of demand and savings deposits, savings and loan shares and government bonds, which amounted to $42.8 billion at the end of 1940, was $133.8 billion at the end of 1949.[2-3]

Not all of this sum — which somewhat exceeds total expenditures for consumers' goods in 1949 — can be thought of as hanging over the market. Part of the $28.3 billion in demand deposits, which are included, is in the process of being spent anyway at any given time. Some of the remaining $105.5 billion is in large holdings which will never be spent for consumers' goods. Nonetheless, one may assume that a considerable part of these spendable assets have been and are still being held off the market by the depression psychosis. They are being held as a protection against a disaster

[2] Excluding trust funds. Federal Reserve *Bulletin*, August 1950, p. 967.

[3] In early 1950 about two thirds of all households had some liquid assets of the above sort. Approximately one household in three had more than $1000; one in eleven had more than $5000. However, about two thirds of all the liquid assets belonged to one tenth of the households. Federal Reserve *Bulletin*, December 1950, pp. 1591 ff.

such as that of the thirties when they would become both necessary and also more valuable.

In the autumn of 1950, for the first time in twenty years, this great stabilizing conviction that a depression is likely to occur sometime in the future was sharply shaken by the Korean war. It was replaced, for many, by the belief that prices would rise for an indefinite period. The federal budget during these months was in balance; the increase in military expenditures as the result of the Korean war was negligible. There occurred, nonetheless, the sharpest price increase in modern American history. Its ultimate cause was the change in the expectations of the public and their consequent efforts to convert spendable assets into goods. The price increase was accelerated by business borrowing and buying for inventory, partly the result of a similar release from the depression psychosis, partly from the need to keep inventories abreast of consumer buying.

The pressure of demand from this source is just as capable as a government deficit of nourishing the continued interaction of prices and wages.

IV

In principle, the Keynesian formula can be brought to bear on price increases resulting from wage-price interaction. Increased taxes and decreased government spending could reduce demand below the amount that is necessary to carry off the current supply of goods. There is also some possibility that, by restricting bank credit, business expenditures for inventories, plant and equipment and consumers' expenditures for durable goods can also be reduced. However, apart from some opportunities for the direct control of consumer credit, this is a far less certain way of reducing spending than by increasing taxes and by reducing public expenditures. (It is precisely for this reason, as the layman viewing controversies between the Treasury and the Federal Reserve System and the bankers should be aware, that it produces the most violent disputes. When one is having the greatest difficulty proving his case, he is always tempted to take refuge in the greatest certainty of statement.)

The effect of reducing the demand for goods is to make it difficult to increase prices. Increasing living costs, in turn, cease to be a pretext or an occasion for wage demands. And, because employers will have greater difficulty in passing wage increase along in prices to the public, they will be resisted.

There are three difficulties with this policy, none of which hamper its counterpart application to deflation and depression. There is first the ineluctable fact that it runs not with, but against, the current of politics. To decrease government expenditures and especially to raise taxes is politically far less agreeable than the reverse — as a myriad of prophets of the commonplace have emphasized. Beyond this is the fact that, while no one makes money out of a depression — a few unvocal *rentiers* and recipients of fixed incomes excepted — inflation is financially to the advantage of important groups in the community. Those whose income moves with prices are, at a minimum, in a protected position and those whose selling prices show a greater than average amplitude of movement gain in real income. In the inflation years of the forties, farmers and recipients of business profits did gain greatly in real income. It is not possible for any reputable American to be overtly in favor of inflation; it is a symbol of evil, like adultery, against which a stand must be taken in public however much it is enjoyed in private. In any case, no person of repute can espouse inflation on behalf of his own income. But the best that can be hoped from this moral ban is neutrality. Those who benefit from inflation cannot be counted upon to be militant proponents of the measures that hold it in check.

The second difficulty, when demand is augmented by pressure of government requirements for things of high urgency, is that only half of the Keynesian formula is available for use and the use of that half may be contradictory and unwise. When the demand that is pressing on the capacity of the economy is for defense or war requirements, it is obviously not possible to relieve this pressure by reducing government expenditures. The spending that is causing the pressure on demand is for something of a higher order of urgency even than stability. Inflation that is being caused by defense spending cannot be checked by reducing defense spending.

Thus, in wartime or when war threatens, the government has only taxation or its equivalent at its disposal.[4] The object of an astringent tax policy, as I have just noted, is to make goods hard to sell — to make it difficult for employers to pass the costs of wage increases along to the public. As a further necessary effect, this policy reduces the demand for labor so that employers are not impelled to surrender to all wage demands in order to hold their labor force. In brief, a strong tax policy works by reducing the pressure of production on capacity.

But in different terms, this means that some plant and some labor must be unemployed. This does not happen in competitive industries, like agriculture, where a new equilibrium of supply and demand with full use of resources will promptly be found at a lower price. It is an absolute and inescapable

---

[4] To the person who asks if civilian expenditures of government can be reduced, the answer is yes. But I am talking here of the aggregate expenditures of government of which military expenditures are a large part of the total at such times.

requirement for stability in industries characterized by a generally developed countervailing power. Some slack in the economy is what keeps countervailing power from being converted into a coalition against the public.

In peacetime the unemployment and idle capacity necessary for stability is not probably of great consequence. Such unemployment is not chronic. Those whom it affects, apart from the fact that they are now protected by greatly improved social security and public welfare assistance, can normally expect re-employment in their regular occupation within a reasonably short time. They can as individuals, with reasonable luck and diligence, find re-employment in another occupation at any time. We are not dealing here with the hopeless idleness of the thirties. An unemployment of four million in mid-1949, which except in a few industries appears to have been enough to rehabilitate countervailing power in the economy, seems to have produced no serious social strains. The discomforts associated with it could be still further minimized by more generous and longer unemployment compensation benefits.

Given the imperatives of defense or of war, however, no such unemployment can be afforded — or at least it will not be afforded. There is certain to be pressure to use the labor force and industrial plant to capacity. The effect of this is to rule out the possibility of achieving stability by high taxation. Although few forms of sport are more favored with us, it is impossible to ride two horses in opposite directions at the same time.

These matters are currently the subject of serious misunderstanding by those who presume to educate the people in the economics of inflation. For months, as I write, Washington officials and business spokesmen have been proclaiming at luncheon meetings and similar tribal rites that "production is the real answer to inflation." A current seven-column advertisement of the life insurance companies carries the banner, "One way to hit at the heart of inflation — more production."

One very elementary point seems to have been overlooked in much of this discussion. When additional goods are produced, additional income, in the form of wages or other payments, also becomes available to buy them. Except for the part of this income that is taxed away or saved, there is an increase in demand to match the increase in supply. But more important, it will now be clear that the pressure of production on the capacity of the industrial plant and labor force, with its effect on the operation of countervailing power, leads directly to inflation. Increased production may be an imperative, but imperative efforts to increase production, so far from being a cure for inflation, are a cause.

If maximum current production is taken as an imperative, then the only paths are either to have open inflation or to remove to central authority the power of decision over prices and wages. Wage and price controls, in the latter instance, rather than a margin of unemployed men and capacity, keep wages from interacting on prices. Demand can then be allowed to press upon the supply of labor and plant in the industries where there is countervailing power up to the point of full use. (It should not, either in principle or practice, be allowed to press further and build up redundant purchasing power behind the controls. A strong tax policy is no less important when there are controls than when there are not. The only difference is that with controls, taxes are no longer expected to achieve ends inconsistent with maximized production.)

A wealthy community like the United States has, in principle, the option of taxing itself heavily enough and thus creating enough slack in markets to sustain considerable defense expenditures without controls. Stability would be purchased, in this manner, not only by a reduction in the standard of living but by a reduction *below* what would be possible were it not necessary to maintain some slack between the capacity of plant and labor force and what is produced. This would require a rare exercise of restraint and economic intelligence. Perhaps it is possible.

In recent times democratic governments in general, and the United States in particular, have opted for control. There can be little doubt that it is preferable to inflation. The social and political effects of open and severe inflation are vicious. Inflation, as a wealth of recent experience shows, destroys the effectiveness and the integrity of government. It afflicts schools, colleges, churches, charitable institutions — in fact all of the amenities which Western man has so laboriously built up and which permit him to describe himself as civilized. It rewards the grossest and most material of talents. No democracy that has experienced a severe or a long-continued inflation has survived wholly intact. But inflation is also inimical to production. It rewards equally the man who produces and the man who holds resources out of production for their appreciation in money value. It draws resources from where they are most needed to serve the wants of those who have most profited. So it, also, is inconsistent with maximum production.

v

I have argued that capitalism, as a practical matter rather than as a system of theology, is an arrangement for getting a considerable decentralization in decision. An examination of the propects for capitalism — of the substance of the fears which the early chapters of this book dug out of the books and the boardrooms — becomes, in the last analysis, an examination of the prospects for decentralized decision. A major danger to decentralized decision has now been isolated. It does not come from depression. Indeed a tendency in this direction must be counted a positive strength. There is, perhaps, no great danger in any inflationary tensions that are likely to be encountered in peacetime. There is the possibility that the depression psychosis might be liquidated by many years of peacetime prosperity, and its effects in stabilizing the ownership of liquid assets thereby lost. More probably, in peacetime, this would operate as a contributory rather than an original cause of inflationary tension.

Given war or preparation for war — coupled with the effect of these on the public's expectations as to prices — there is every likelihood that the scope for decentralized decision will be substantially narrowed. It is inflation, not deflation or depression, that will cause capitalism to be modified by extensive centralized decision. The position of capitalism in face of this threat is exceedingly vulnerable. This is not a matter of theory but of experience. In the autumn of 1950 a secondary military operation in a country thousands of miles away was sufficient to bring about a wholesale centralization. A few months of inflation accomplished what ten years of depression had not required. For twenty years Americans who hold to the doctrine of the malignant state had suspected that New Dealers and Fair Dealers had in mind some such design for American capitalism. In the event the action was forced on the Administration by an essentially conservative Congress.

The centralization of decision which is necessary to compensate for the disappearance of countervailing power as a stabilizing force in inflation is much less comprehensive than what is associated with, say, public ownership. Our experience with it is limited; one can only guess about its ultimate consequences. Perhaps if it is coupled with a tax policy that keeps redundant demand from building up behind the controls — if the regulations are limited to their indispensable purpose which is to allow maximum production without having wages interact with prices — the effects may not be far-reaching. Given good will and good humor — two essential and sadly deficient ingredients of good government — the outlook would be even better. But no one can doubt that inflationary tensions are capable of bringing a major revision in the character and constitution of American capitalism. If the world is fortunate enough to find peace then the prospect is a good deal brighter.

INDEX

INDEX

A & P (Great Atlantic & Pacific Tea Co.), 125, 126, 128, 132, 148
Adelman, M. A., 125, 148 n.
Advertising, 50
  consumer's goods industries, 104–5
  and competition, 105–7
  and wealth, 102–7
Agriculture, employment in, 110. *See also* Farmers
Agricultural Adjustment Act of 1933, 155, 168
Agricultural Marketing Act of 1929, 167
Agricultural Marketing Agreement Act of 1937, 145
American Tobacco Co. v. *United States*, 56
Antitrust, 55–56, 58
  and businessmen, 64–65
  and countervailing power, 149–51
  and market power, 62–63
  and public regulation, 58–59
  and farmers, 163–65

and large retail firms, 147–49
Anti-Trust Division, Department of Justice, 56
Arnold, Thurman, 7, 56

Baer, George F., 64
Bain, Joe S., 43 n.
Barone, Enrico, 17
Basing point system, 135
  and countervailing power, 128
Bentham, Jeremy, 1, 32
Berle, Adolf A., 40
Beveridge, Sir William, 23, 24 n.
Biddle, Nicholas, 162 n.
Big Business
  conflict with competition, 39
  concentration of ownership, 36–37
  importance of, 40, 41
  industry concentration, 42, 43
  investigations of, 36
Bituminous Coal Conservation Act of 1935, 142